THE LIVING CONSTITUTION

THE · WORKERS · BOOKSHELF

The Living Constitution

A CONSIDERATION OF THE REALITIES AND LEGENDS OF OUR FUNDAMENTAL LAW

By HOWARD LEE MCBAIN ~ ~ ~
The Ruggles Professor of Constitutional Law in Columbia University ~ ~ ~

Published by THE WORKERS EDUCATION BUREAU PRESS *at 476 West 24th. Street,* New York City ~ ~ ~ ~ 1927

Copyright, 1927
WORKERS EDUCATION BUREAU PRESS, INC.

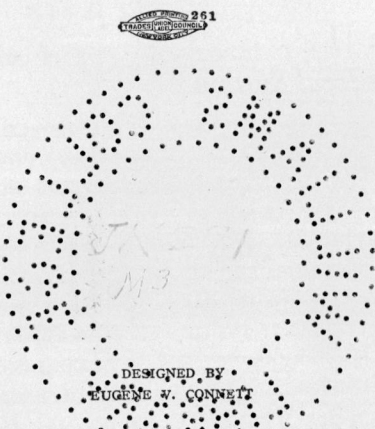

Printed in the United States
under union conditions

CONTENTS

Chapter I 1
Written Constitutions

LAWS AND MEN—THE LIFE OF THE LAW—RULES OF THE GAME—OUR MANIFOLD LAWS—WHAT IS A CONSTITUTION—AMERICAN CONSTITUTION—WRITTEN AND UNWRITTEN CONSTITUTIONS—FLEXIBLE AND RIGID CONSTITUTIONS—AMENDING THE AMERICAN CONSTITUTION—AMENDING STATE CONSTITUTIONS—CUSTOMS OF THE CONSTITUTION—STATUTES AND THE CONSTITUTION—COURTS AND THE CONSTITUTION.

Chapter II 34
The Federal System

FEDERAL AND UNITARY SYSTEMS—CONSENT OF STATES—LIMITED OR UNLIMITED POWERS—NATIONAL INVASION OF STATE POWERS—COMMERCE POWER—IMPOTENCE OF STATES—ENCROACHMENT ON STATES—INCONSISTENCIES—NATIONAL POLICE POWERS—EXAMPLES OF POLICE POWER LAWS—LIQUOR LAWS—SUMMARY OF EFFECTS—SERVICES-IN-AID — GRANTS-IN-AID — FEDERALISM AND NATIONALISM—REASONS FOR FEDERALISM—STATES' RIGHTS—PROBLEM OF FEDERAL DIVISION.

Chapter III 72
Bills of Rights

WHAT ARE BILLS OF RIGHTS—PRIVATE RIGHT

CONTENTS

V. PUBLIC POWER—PRIVATE RIGHTS AND DUE PROCESS—PRIVATE RIGHTS UNDER CONTRACT CLAUSE—NEED FOR BILL OF RIGHTS—TREASON AND FREE SPEECH—ESPIONAGE ACT—HABEAS CORPUS—HABEAS CORPUS IN WAR TIME—PROHIBITION AND BILL OF RIGHTS—SEARCHES AND SEIZURES—JURY TRIAL—PADLOCK PRACTISE—DOUBLE JEOPARDY—DUE PROCESS OF LAW—CHANGING BILLS OF RIGHTS.

CHAPTER IV.. 114

The Presidential System

PRESIDENT AS CHIEF LEGISLATOR—PRESIDENT AS CHIEF EXECUTIVE—CABINET AS LEADER OF LEGISLATION—CHOICE OF PRESIDENTIAL LEADER—CHOICE OF PRIME MINISTER—BRITISH AND AMERICAN CONTRASTS—SOURCE OF PRESIDENT'S POWER—SOURCE OF CABINET'S POWER—PRESIDENTIAL RESPONSIBILITY — CABINET RESPONSIBILITY — RECENT BRITISH ELECTIONS—OUR CLOCKLIKE ELECTIONS—PRESIDENTIAL SYSTEM ASSESSED—PROPOSED REFORM.

CHAPTER V.. 150

Checks and Balances

LORD BRYCE'S VIEW—THE FATHERS' INTENTION—ARE CHECKS UNDEMOCRATIC—THE CHECK OF COURTS—THE SUPREME COURT AND CHILD LABOR—CHECK OF TWO CHAMBERS—DECLINE OF SECOND CHAMBERS—SENATE AND HOUSE—POWER OF VETO—CHECK OF POWER TO APPOINT—HISTORY

CONTENTS

OF POWER TO REMOVE—THE 1926 DECISION—WHAT WILL CONGRESS DO—WHAT WILL THE PRESIDENT DO—CHECK ON TREATY MAKING—AMENDING TREATIES—SURVIVAL OF CHECKS.

CHAPTER VI 202

The Representative System

AIMS OF REPRESENTATION—IDEALISM AND PRACTICAL POLITICS—LOCAL VS. NATIONAL REPRESENTATION—THEORY AND FACTS—REPRESENTATION BY GEOGRAPHICAL DISTRICTS—EQUALITY OF REPRESENTATION—REPRESENTATION IN THE SENATE—WILSON ON THE SENATE—PROPORTIONAL REPRESENTATION—CONSENT OF THE GOVERNED.

CHAPTER VII 237

Judicial Control

ORIGIN OF JUDICIAL CONTROL—MARSHALL'S VIEW—APPLIED TO ACTS OF CONGRESS—APPLIED TO STATE ACTS—VETO BY STATE COURTS—JUDICIAL VETO IN HISTORY—RECENT ATTACKS—REFORM PROPOSALS—FIVE TO FOUR DECISIONS—CONTEMPT OF COURT—GOVERNMENT BY INJUNCTION—CLAYTON ACT—CONTEMPT POWER IN GENERAL.

CHAPTER VIII 272

In Conclusion

BIBLIOGRAPHICAL NOTE 275

INDEX 281

Chapter I

Written Constitutions

THE Declaration of Rights in the Massachusetts constitution of 1780 concluded with a famous phrase. The legislative, executive, and judicial powers were to be in separate hands, it was written, "to the end that" the government of this commonwealth "may be a government of laws and not of men." In the year 1921 Mr. Chief Justice Taft, in an opinion which he read for the United States Supreme Court, quoted this phrase as a maxim showing the spirit in which our laws are expected to be made and applied. There was something of unconscious irony in this. For the law that was involved in that case was an Arizona statute which prohibited Arizona judges from issuing injunctions to prevent "peaceful picketing" in time of strikes. The Chief Justice and four of his associates held the act void because in their judgment it denied the equal protection of the laws to employers whose employees were on strike. But in the opinion of the four other mem-

Laws and Men

THE LIVING CONSTITUTION

bers of the Court the law was not invalid. Was this five to four decision of the Supreme Court the act of a government of laws and not of men? Manifestly not. For judges are men, usually able and conscientious men to be sure, but made of human stuff like the rest of us and sharing with us the common limitations and frailties of human nature. This law was unmade by five men—in a sense, indeed, by the one man who cast the fifth and deciding vote.

"Away with the cant of 'Measures, not men!'" shouted Mr. Canning in 1801,—"the idle supposition that it is the harness and not the horses that draw the chariot along. No, sir; if the comparison must be made, if the distinction must be taken, men are everything, measures are comparatively nothing." Here we have the opposite of the Massachusetts maxim, a declaration for a government of men and not of laws.

Both of these expressions contain truth and error. All governments are governments of men as well as of laws; for government is a human institution. Laws are man-made, man-executed, man-interpreted. Sometimes the laws, sometimes the men, seem the more important to us; and whether the one or the other often depends upon whether

WRITTEN CONSTITUTIONS

we agree or disagree with the manner in which men interpret and apply the laws. No doubt the Arizona employers looked upon the above-mentioned decision as a vindication of government by law, for it affirmed the supremacy of the law of the national constitution over the law of the state legislature. No doubt the employees looked upon it as an act of a government of men, for five men annulled a law which four of their colleagues thought should have been sustained.

The truth of the matter is that under democratic conditions it is absurd to strike a complete contrast between a government of laws and a government of men. Laws are the product, men the producers. Strictly speaking the two are not comparable. Laws without men to interpret and enforce them have neither life nor purpose. We speak of the "living" body of the law, but this is mere metaphor. The life of the law is a borrowed life. It is, like the life of man's other material and intellectual products, borrowed from the life of man. Laws live only because men live and only to the extent that men will to have them live. Apart from men a government of laws is a thing inert, a thing that is harmless because useless, a thing that has no existence outside the realm of imagination.

The Life of the Law

THE LIVING CONSTITUTION

For all practical purposes a government of men without laws is likewise inconceivable. If, as Proudhon said, "the true form of the state is anarchy," nowhere yet has the state run true to form. People in association either desire or acquiesce in authority; and almost of necessity the exercise of authority over a numerous group implies laws. It is easier all around, both for the governors and the governed. It is mere common sense.

It is, therefore, only in a relative sense, only in point of degree, that the phrases "government of laws" and "government of men" have meaning. *Rules of the Game* The one connotes a government in which the governed are told in advance what the rules of the game of living together are. Generally speaking, therefore, they know what the rules are and they know whether or not they are conforming to them and what to expect if they are apprehended in violating them. But the rules are numerous. They are not always perfectly definite. Some of them are written in very general terms. Some of them are extremely complicated. Moreover the human relationships which they seek to control are often highly complex and vary widely in detail of circumstance. It is, in consequence, indispensable that the rules should be construed and applied to spe-

[4]

WRITTEN CONSTITUTIONS

cific sets of facts by officials, judges, and juries. To the extent that this is necessary a government of laws becomes also a government of men. Even so, the laws are far more important and permanent than the men. Injustice may occasionally result—does in fact occasionally result under all man-operated governments. Yet arbitrary departure from the established rules is exceptional.

A government of men, on the other hand, implies a government in which the emphasis is reversed. There may be rules of conduct, but the rules are less important than the men who interpret and apply them. It implies a capricious and arbitrary and unequal construction of such rules as exist, a disregard of precedent, an application of new and special rules created out of hand and after the fact. Injustice and unfairness are, or at least may be, the rule rather than the exception. The governed do not and cannot know approximately where they stand under the law.

The difference, then, between a government of laws and a government of men (to the extent that these phrases have any real meaning) is not a difference in kind but a difference of degree only. It is nevertheless a difference of high and important degree; for it bespeaks a difference in spirit;

and in government as in most other human institutions the spirit is often the essence.

In the limited sense just defined the American government is of a certainty a government of laws. No other people on earth is or ever has been governed under so many and such elaborate laws as we acquiesce and apparently rejoice in. We have our national constitution, the fundamental law of the nation; and under this Congress has enacted innumerable statutes. Each of the forty-eight states has its own constitution; and under these fundamental laws our legislative mills (in most states biennially, in a few states annually) turn out a grist of statutes the bulk of which is truly appalling. Each of our thousands of cities has its charter, which being its fundamental law is in the nature of a "constitution" for the city; and under these charters city councils are endlessly engaged in enacting local laws or ordinances.

Our Manifold Laws

It is of course easy to give a grossly exaggerated picture of this amplitude of our laws by amassing for the entire country the huge figures showing the number of laws or the number of pages of laws enacted. We are told, for example, that more than 11,000 statutes were put on the books in the single year 1925, even though in six states the legisla-

WRITTEN CONSTITUTIONS

ture did not meet in that year. Such big figures mean little. For generally speaking the only laws that are applicable to any individual are the laws of the nation, of his own state, and of his own local community. They are not the laws of the country as a whole. With the laws of states and localities other than his own the individual has no concern except that some of these laws apply to him when he is on travel or owns property or carries on a business beyond the jurisdiction of his residence. But viewed in the most favorable light none of us has reason to complain of a dearth of written rules for our governance. In point of number of rules ours is superlatively a government of laws.

In the matter of relative importance, of superiority and inferiority, these manifold laws are arrayed in something of a hierarchy. At the pinnacle stands the national constitution, the capstone of our entire system or scheme of government. It is to this, our most important law, that our chief attention will be directed.

Every country in the world is governed under something that may be called a constitution. But these constitutions vary enormously in point of historical origin, of form, of content, of tangibility, of stability, of permanence. For this reason it is

What is a Constitu-[tion?

difficult to define a constitution accurately and comprehensively. Though publicists and jurists have not been reluctant to hazard definitions, it is easier to puncture these with criticism than it is to improve upon them. Consider a few of them:

Justice Joseph Story, one of the great commentators on the American constitution, wrote that "a constitution is a fundamental law or basis of government . . . established by the people in their original capacity". But the constitutions of many countries are not established by the people—the people only acquiesce in them; and "sovereign" is at best a most obstreperous and baffling word. The same objection lodges against Justice Paterson's definition written in 1795: A constitution "is a form of government, delineated by the mighty hand of the people, in which certain first principles of fundamental laws are established". At a much later date Judge Cooley, another eminent American commentator, defined a constitution as "the fundamental law of the state, containing the principles upon which government is founded, regulating the division of the sovereign powers and directing to what persons each of these powers is to be confided and the manner in which it is to be exercised". Apart from the vagueness of the

WRITTEN CONSTITUTIONS

phrase "sovereign powers", it is simply a fact that many constitutions do not direct to what persons every one of the powers of government is to be confided, to say nothing of determining the manner in which every power is to be exercised.

The well-known English author of *The American Commonwealth*, the late Lord Bryce, described the constitution of a state or nation as consisting "of those of its rules or laws which determine the form of its government and the respective rights and duties of it toward its citizens and of the citizen toward the government". But there are many constitutions which contain little or nothing concerning the reciprocal rights and duties of government and citizen toward each other. And much the same criticism may be made of the definition of Charles Borgeaud, a distinguished French authority: "A constitution is the fundamental law according to which the government of a state is organized and agreeably to which the relations of individuals or moral persons to the community are determined."

No doubt the genius of so living and diversified a thing as government abhors nicety of definition. Certain it is that a constitution, generically conceived, does not lend itself to ready definition. It will be observed, however, that one word rings through nearly all of these definitions, and through many others that might be quoted, the word "fundamental". Whatever else a constitution is it is fundamental. It lies at the bottom; it is foundation; all else in law and in government is superstructure, however important it may be.

We have said that among all our laws our national constitution stands at the prinnacle. This sounds like paradox. How can a law both stand at the top and lie at the bottom? But the paradox is only apparent; we have simply altered metaphors. When we speak of its superiority over all other laws we personify it. It is above and controls all others. When we speak of its fundamentality we refer to it in terms of structure. It is below and supports all others, which must conform to its foundational lines. It thus happens that the phrase "the supreme law of the land"—the topmost— and the phrase "the fundamental law of the land" —the bottommost—are constantly used interchangeably. There is in this no inconsistency.

We may, then, it would seem, advantageously abandon any attempt to define constitutions in general. There is in fact a deal of useless lingo in the literature of the so-called social sciences. Everybody knows in a general way what a constitution is even though he may not be able to fuse the sense of his concept into impregnable words.

As for the American constitution we may for practical purposes say that it is the document, as amended and interpreted to date, which was drafted by a famous convention sitting in Philadelphia in the year 1787, which was ratified by conventions called for that purpose in the several states, and which went into effect in 1789. We say it is this document "as amended and interpreted to date"; for nineteen formal amendments have been added to the constitution since 1789, although ten of these were adopted immediately thereafter and may therefore be regarded as part of the original instrument. And wholly apart from amendments by which the actual words of the constitution have been altered or added to, a living constitution cannot remain static. Our constitution has, as we shall see, developed by the growth of custom, by the practices of political parties, by the action or inaction of Congress or the President, and especially by judicial interpretation.

American Constitution

The national constitution establishes our federal system of government by enumerating the powers of the national government and reserving generally all other powers to the states. It provides in outline the main branches of the national government and broadly distributes powers among them. The government is limited by the rule that it can exercise only the powers that are expressly or impliedly conferred upon it. Moreover, the constitution also contains, especially in the first eight amendments, a series of prohibitions upon the government in behalf of individual rights. Upon these rights, even in the exercise of its granted powers, the government is, as we shall see, forbidden to encroach.

The national constitution sets up the framework of a government that is within its sphere complete. But considering the governmental needs of the country as a whole, its sphere is by no means complete. It could not operate at all unless the state governments also operated. It not only assumes the continued existence of the states but also imposes upon them a few very important, and in some instances very vaguely phrased, restrictions. Subject to these restrictions and to the general rule that the states may not infringe upon any power expressly or impliedly given to the national government, each state frames and adopts a constitution for its own government. In turn these constitutions, varying widely in length, scope, and date of adoption, provide the principal organs and distribute generally the powers of the state governments. They likewise impose numerous positive and negative restrictions upon these governments.

The national constitution and the constitutions of the forty-eight states, complementing each other, form the basis of our constitutional system.

In discussing constitutions it has long been customary to call attention to the distinction between written and unwritten constitutions and to contrast such a constitution as that of Great Britain with that of the United States. The American constitution is a written document, somewhat altered by unwritten custom or precedent and very largely reshaped and expanded as to some of its parts by written statutes and judicial opinions. The British constitution, as Lord Bryce put it, "is a mass of precedents carried in men's minds or recorded in writing, dicta of lawyers and statesmen, customs, usages, understandings and beliefs, a number of statutes mixed up with customs and all covered with a parasitic growth of legal decisions and political habits." It is formless, dateless, elusive. It was not "struck off by the mind and heart of man", as Mr. Gladstone once said of the Amer-

Written and Unwritten Constitutions

ican constitution. It has simply grown. Nevertheless, difficult as it may be to collate the statutes that go into its partial making, the British constitution has for some time been growing far more rapidly and importantly by the process of enacting written statutes than it has by the process of altering customs or conventions.

Moreover, the British constitution is both the first and the last of its kind. Every other important state in the world and most unimportant states are now governed under constitutions that are primarily written. The tendency in this direction has been almost unexceptional since the adoption of the American constitution and since the "declaration of the rights of man" that preceded the French Revolution. The sundering of Europe at the close of the World War only added impetus. Hungary alone excepted, all of the new states which rose on the ruins of Russia, Austria-Hungary, and Germany adopted written constitutions.

Nor is this surprising. The people of the American colonies in 1776, of France in 1789, of Russia in 1917, of the collapsed central empires in 1918, were torn from the mooring of traditional monarchy. In such circumstances it was impossible for them to sit quietly and resolve that they would

WRITTEN CONSTITUTIONS

be governed under an unwritten, a customary, a traditional constitution. The one essential tradition around which such a constitution could develop was lacking; the monarchy was gone. England has had her revolutions, but her monarchy has survived them. Her central and most important outward "convention" has remained. And this also may be said: had not the spirit of liberty awakened in the English and asserted itself at an early date, had *Magna Charta* been "wrested" from the king in the late eighteenth or early nineteenth century instead of in 1215, that document would in all probability have contained more than an assertion of certain civil rights of the individual and a denunciation of the abuses of the king as feudal superior. It would have been a written constitution, somewhat similar no doubt to those which were "wrested" from numerous princes of the continent during the first half of the last century.

It is idle, therefore, to discuss the relative merits of written and unwritten constitutions, as if people could ordinarily make a choice between the one and the other. The unwritten British constitution, to the extent that it is unwritten, is due less to peculiar institutional genius than to historical accident. The written constitutions of most other coun-

THE LIVING CONSTITUTION

tries are due to force of circumstances. What else could the people do but write fundamental laws for their governance?

Flexible and Rigid Constitu-[tions

It is customary also, since Lord Bryce suggested the terms, to distinguish between flexible and rigid constitutions, the difference depending upon the ease or difficulty with which constitutions may be temporarily or permanently altered. The distinction is not, or at least should not be, based upon the written or unwritten character of the constitution. The unwritten British constitution is nevertheless usually cited as the example *par excellence* of a flexible constitution. Is it so in fact?

If we put aside the period of the late war when all constitutions, including the American, flexed rather perceptibly, it is open to doubt whether in practise the British constitution can be said to yield readily to change. In the introduction to the second edition of his masterly work on *The English Constitution*, Mr. Walter Bagehot spoke of the "many changes, some of spirit and some of detail," that had been wrought upon the constitution in the brief span of years between 1865 and 1872. There had in fact been one and only one change of importance—the extension of the suffrage by the Reform Act of 1867. And even in his discussion

WRITTEN CONSTITUTIONS

of this Mr. Bagehot dwelt upon its political rather than its constitutional aspects. For the rest he spoke of potential, not actual, alterations—of the curtailment of the powers of the House of Lords, which did not arrive until 1911; of the submission of treaties to the approval of Parliament, which did not arrive until the Treaty of Versailles.

The fact is that, while a number of minor modifications may be noted, the British constitution has been changed in but few important particulars in the course of a near-century; and most of these came about not with any swift and sudden yielding of a flexible instrument but after years of agitation for, and rigid resistance to, reform. It required a far longer and fiercer struggle to carry woman's suffrage into the Representation of the People's Act of 1918 than was found necessary to sweep the Susan B. Anthony Amendment into the "rigid" constitution of the United States. In spite of gross inequalities of representation resulting in heavy disfranchisement of the crowded industrial centers, there was no redistribution of seats in the House of Commons from 1885 to 1918—a period of thirty-three years. The apparently sudden retrenchment of the powers of the Lords in 1909–11 had been ripe for years. It only awaited their first important failure to heed Mr. Bagehot's admonition of 1872 that they "ought, on a first-class subject, to be slow—very slow—in rejecting a bill passed even once by a large majority of the House of Commons". The noose into which they slipped their noble heads had long been prepared by the inexorable logic of the constitution itself. Of the length of the furious battle which culminated in the setting up of the Irish Free State little need be said. If the constitution has bent easily to the changed and changing status of the self-governing dominions in foreign affairs, this has been the flexibility of fear. No; in matters of importance the British constitution is flexible only in theory. It is certainly no more flexible than are many if not most written constitutions.

No one denies, of course, that British politics has changed enormously in the course of a century. Partly as a result of the several extensions of the suffrage and partly due to the rise of the powerful Labor Party, the grip of the "governing class" has slipped and is still slipping. For better or worse British politics is, so to say, being "Americanized". But politics is one thing and the constitution is another. The fact that the American Senate has in the last two or three decades changed radically

WRITTEN CONSTITUTIONS

in the quality and caliber of its personnel, from whatever cause arising, we do not regard as a constitutional change.

If we ignore for the moment modifications and expansions by custom and interpretation, written constitutions vary in the matter of their resistance to change. Some are flexible, some are less so. The constitution of the United States has been regarded as peculiarly rigid—an oft-decried feature of our system. Merely to propose an amendment a two-thirds vote of each house of Congress is necessary —an extraordinary majority not easily secured. And the proposal must then be ratified by the legislatures in three-fourths of the states. This means the affirmative vote of seventy-four different legislative bodies—the two houses of Congress and the two houses of thirty-six state legislatures. On paper it reads like a wholly unworkable scheme except perhaps in the presence of an overwhelming popular demand. Until the adoption of the sixteenth amendment in 1913 many commentators declared that for practical purposes our constitution had become unamendable. History seemed to bear this out. Since 1804—a lapse of more than a century—no amendment had been added to the constitution except the three that were born out

Amending the American Constitu-[tion

of the sanguinary travail of the Civil War. Suddenly the spell was broken as if by magic. In the eight years from 1913 to 1920 four amendments were adopted, providing respectively for the income tax, popular election of United States senators, prohibition, and woman's suffrage. Moreover, strange to relate, it can scarcely be said that the latter two were backed by an overwhelmingly favorable sentiment of the people of the country as a whole. One of them, however, the prohibition amendment, was carried during the hectic hysteria of the war. At any rate the American constitution can no longer be regarded as unamendable.

It ought also to be said that, so far as experience discloses, the crux of the rigidity of the American amending process lies in the two-thirds vote required of the Senate and the House of Representatives. It is Congress that smothers proposed amendments in its own bosom. Of the twenty-four that have been actually passed by Congress only five have been defeated because of failure of the states to ratify. The proposed child labor amendment was the latest and most important to suffer that fate. This is not to say, however, that had Congress been more prolific in the matter of proposals, the stiff requirement of ratification by three-fourths of the states might not have proved to be a most formidable obstacle. Whether it would or would not have been such is wholly conjectural.

Curiously enough the difficulty of the process of amending a constitution does not appear in practise to have much to do with whether amendments are actually adopted or not. Other things seem to control. Under the constitution of the old German Empire an amendment required an ordinary majority of the Reichstag and a more than three-fourths vote of the Bundesrath. During its forty-seven years of life (1871–1918) fourteen amendments were adopted. In France constitutional amendments may be adopted by a process almost as simple as that employed for the enactment of ordinary statutes; yet since the adoption of the constitution in 1875 but six amendments have been added, that of 1926 being the only amendment since 1884. The fact that amendments have been few certainly cannot be credited to the perfection of the constitutional laws of France or of the system of government for which they provide.

Among the constitutions of the several American states the amending process varies considerably. Complete details cannot be given here. A majority of them require a two-thirds or a three-

THE LIVING CONSTITUTION

Amending State Constitu-[tions

fifths vote of each house of the legislature and subsequent ratification at the polls. But if practice be considered, this is no criterion of rigidity. In spite of such a requirement the number of amendments to the ludicrously lengthy constitution of Louisiana, which dates only from 1913, runs well over the hundred mark. On the other hand the Utah constitution of 1895, with a similar requirement, has been amended less than a score of times. The California constitution which went into effect in 1879 was amended very freely under the requirement of a two-thirds vote even prior to the adoption in 1911 of the additional mode of amendment by initiative and referendum. In all more than a hundred and fifty amendments have been ratified in that state in less than fifty years.

About one fourth of the states prescribe that amendments shall be passed by two successive legislatures (some of these require also an extraordinary majority vote) and thereafter be approved by the people. This seems like a fairly difficult process; but again practise fails to establish it as a test of rigidity. Under this system the constitution of New York, a not unconservative state, has been amended more than thirty times since 1894; but the constitution of Iowa records fewer than twenty

WRITTEN CONSTITUTIONS

amendments since 1857—a period of seventy years. During this long interval this state has experienced at least occasional waves of radicalism.

These few figures are not conclusive. They do, however, seem to point the danger of measuring the inflexibility of a constitution solely by the verbal yardstick of its amending process. Why does the two-thirds amending rule operate with such oiled facility in Baton Rouge, Louisiana, or in Sacramento, California, and with such viscous difficulty in Washington, D. C.? Many reasons for the difference are patent. They are not important here. The point is merely that the flexibility of the one and the relative rigidity of the other constitution derive from factors that lie largely, if not wholly, outside the letter of the amending process.

It must be said, however, that the unadaptive quality of a few of our state constitutions is directly chargeable to peculiarly hard requirements in the matter of amendments; as in New Hampshire where amendments may not be proposed by the legislature at all but only by a constitutional convention; as in Montana where not more than three amendments may be submitted at one election; as in New Jersey and Pennsylvania where amendments may be submitted not oftener than once in five years (in Tennessee and Vermont, once in six and in ten years respectively); as in Illinois where amendments may be proposed to only one article of the constitution at a time and to the same article not oftener than once in four years and must be approved by a majority of all those voting *at* the election. With the possible exception of New Jersey the figures for amendments in these states, when compared with those having less exacting requirements, prove the obstructive efficacy of these requirements. Illinois, for instance, takes high honors in rigidity, with a record of only seven amendments carried since 1870. This shows impediment beyond all reason.

On the general subject of flexible and rigid constitutions one other point deserves mention. In countries in which the courts do not enjoy the power to declare acts of the legislature void because of conflict with the written constitution—and outside of the United States such power is exercised in very few countries—the question whether or not a written constitution yields easily to formal amendment is not of so great importance as it is with us. For the legislature is the final judge of what is and is not constitutional. While legislatures in such countries do not often flagrantly over-

WRITTEN CONSTITUTIONS

ride the unmistakable prescriptions of their constitutions, they do enact many laws which, if enacted in the United States, would probably be declared invalid by the courts. In this power of the legislature to put its own interpretation upon the constitution there inheres, then, an obvious and significant degree of elasticity. The written constitution becomes in consequence more nearly assimilable in flexibility to the unwritten, whose malleability is, in theory at least, without limit.

State constitutions in the United States have developed—have in other words kept approximate pace with changes in our economic and social life and in our political thinking—chiefly by the process of periodic general revision and by the further process of piecemeal amendment. Not so our national constitution. It has never been generally revised. It carries only nineteen formal amendments. But it *has* developed. It has been altered and enlarged by several different methods. These can be merely illustrated at this point. Some of them will be discussed more fully later.

Customs of the Constitution

The constitution has developed by the growth of customs and especially the customs or practises of political parties. There are a number of well-known examples of this. The constitution decrees that the President shall be chosen by groups of electors in the several states. Thus did the Fathers think to exalt this office above debasing partisan antagonisms. But political parties early decreed otherwise. Candidates are nominated by parties and the electors chosen thereafter merely rubberstamp these nominations. The form remains; the substance has long since passed into limbo. Tradition, not the constitution, prescribes that a President may not be reëlected for a third term. The President's Cabinet, which varies in influence from President to President, is unknown to the fundamental law. The constitution ordains that the President shall "nominate and, by and with the advice and consent of the Senate, shall appoint" officers. The President has never taken the advice of the Senate in the matter of appointments; but party practise ordains that, as to federal officers in the several states, the President shall not only take but also follow the advice of the senator or senators of his own party, if any, from the state in which the appointment is to be made. The senator, not the President, makes the nomination. The constitution is silent as to the power of removal; but from the beginning the President has exercised this power on an extensive scale.

WRITTEN CONSTITUTIONS

The constitution makes the President the chief executive of the nation. In political practise candidates for this high office stand before the people upon a program consisting largely of legislative proposals; and a President seeking reëlection is held to account far more usually upon his legislative than upon his executive record. This is perhaps the most significant of all the "customs of the constitution" that have been wrought upon it by the impious hands of political parties.

Prior to the adoption in 1913 of the amendment providing for popular election of United States senators, numerous states by primary laws had in fact deprived their legislatures of the power to choose senators, a power expressly granted to them by the national constitution. As a result the nation in 1908 witnessed the curious spectacle of a Republican legislature in Oregon electing a Democrat to the United States Senate. The constitution does not require that congressmen shall be residents of the districts of their election; but party practise does so require.

The fourteenth amendment commands that whenever any state denies or abridges the rights of any adult male citizen to vote, the representation of that state in the lower house of Congress shall be proportionately reduced. This provision was still-born in 1868; it has never been vivified. The fifteenth amendment asserts that the right to vote shall not be denied because of race, color, or previous condition of servitude. By various indirect methods this provision, once alive, has by the Southern states been effectively sentenced to "hang by the neck until dead". Thus have these two provisions, forced upon the "conquered provinces" of the South by the no doubt "blessed" but certainly misguided "peacemakers" of the eighteen-sixties, been brought to no avail.

The eighteenth amendment declares that Congress and the several states shall have concurrent power to enforce by appropriate legislation the prohibition of the manufacture, sale, or transportation of intoxicating liquors. Two states, New York and Maryland, "concur" in this by not enacting any enforcement law. And rumor has it that actual enforcement, whether by federal or state agencies, leaves in many states a relatively large margin of the unachieved.

These, then, are some of the customs or conventions of the American constitution, by which this or that provision has been added, expanded, contracted, perverted, or even wholly nullified. They

WRITTEN CONSTITUTIONS

"constitute", as is obvious, a not unimportant part of our constitutional system.

The constitution has also developed by act of Congress or by the action of one or the other house of Congress. Thus the provision of the constitution relating to the counting of the votes of presidential electors in the presence of the Senate and the House is, as one expositor has put it with unintended humor, "pregnant with omissions". Congress has supplied these omissions by an elaborate and rather slovenly law enacted in 1886, ten years after the Tilden-Hayes controversy first disclosed this deficiency of the fundamental law. Again the constitution makes each house the judge of the "qualifications" of its own members; and although the constitution itself prescribes the qualifications, the houses have on occasion exercised the power both of adding to and subtracting from these qualifications. In 1900 the House refused to seat a duly elected member from Utah, who, being a Mormon, had too many wives. In one or two instances the Senate has seated persons who, being a little short of the prescribed age of thirty, were not, as it were, constitutionally adult for the Senate. Repeatedly, moreover, committees of both houses, and especially of the Senate, exercise inquisitorial

Statutes and the Constitution

power over witnesses that is of dubious constitutionality. But this opens a large question, mixed of law, of the rights of witnesses, and of the rights of the public, which cannot be entered here.

In a much more important way, however, than anything yet mentioned has the constitution been developed by Congress. We usually speak of the huge development of our constitution by judicial interpretation. Everything, right or wrong, is laid on the doorstep of the courts, and especially of the Supreme Court. But the courts have nothing to interpret, nothing to develop, until Congress or the state legislatures have acted. Legislative interpretation, legislative development, of the constitution comes first. And nobody can assess the complete effect of the system. It is impossible to say how many laws are enacted by Congress and the state legislatures in the disguised hope and belief that they will be declared unconstitutional by the courts. No one knows how many proposed laws fail of enactment because of genuine conviction that they would be declared void if enacted. On the face of the result, however, we owe our vast expansion of federal powers, particularly under the elastic commerce clause, primarily to Congress. The courts have merely followed where

WRITTEN CONSTITUTIONS

Congress has led; they have merely permitted what Congress has prescribed.

Nor is this all. Whatever limitations have been imposed by the courts on attempted exertions of power by Congress are as nothing compared with the limitations that Congress has by inaction imposed upon itself. There is probably an immense realm of regulatory power which Congress might with the sanction of the courts constitutionally occupy, but which, wisely or unwisely, Congress has as yet not seen fit to occupy. Action by Congress in the years ahead will unquestionably prove this.

In a very real sense, therefore, may it be said that the constitution has been developed by act of Congress. If the Fathers could rise from their graves they would find today much that would seem familiar in the organization and jurisdiction of the federal courts. They would find in the procedure of the two houses a combination of the familiar and the exotic. In the matter of regulatory laws, however, and the stupendous administrative organization that has been evolved for their enforcement, they could not possibly recognize the child of their intellectual parentage. And this gradual transformation has been brought about almost wholly by acts of Congress.

THE LIVING CONSTITUTION

Courts and the Constitution

Nearly all the laws of Congress by which the physiognomy of the constitution has been materially or even slightly altered have been contested before the courts. In the body of these laws there is usually no mention of the constitution, although in the process of enacting them there is commonly high, and sometimes very able, debate upon points of constitutionality. But when these laws reach the courts the judges in their written opinions discuss at great length the meaning of the words and phrases of the constitution. Now the record of Congress that is of chief importance is the law itself. This is printed in the statute books and is thus completely severed from the record of the investigations, the reports, the debates, that may have attended upon its enactment. The record of the court is of course its judgment of the validity or invalidity of the law as applied to a particular set of facts. But this record is closely coupled with the arguments employed and the reasons advanced for the conclusion reached. The opinion and the judgment are printed together in the volumes of the reports of cases decided. Though legally speaking the opinion and the judgment are separable, they are in fact part and parcel of a single pronouncement by the court. And thus they appear.

WRITTEN CONSTITUTIONS

The record, therefore, is filled with declarations that this or that word or phrase or clause of the constitution means or does not mean thus and so. Moreover, the court has the last word upon the subject. Its declaration of meaning is final, unless it is changed by some subsequent declaration made by the court itself.

It is because of this nature of their records and this finality of their adjudications that we think and speak of the courts, and especially of the United States Supreme Court, as being the principal agency by which our written constitution has been and is being developed. As expounders of the constitution their role has truly been of great significance in the unfolding of our institutional life.

"A word", says Mr. Justice Holmes, "is the skin of an idea." As applied to the words of a living constitution the expression is peculiarly apt; for living skin is elastic, expansile, and is constantly being renewed. The constitution of the United States contains only about six thousand words; but millions of words have been written by the courts in elucidation of the ideas these few words encase. Under the magic of judicial interpretation the constitution is neither an Ethiopian nor yet a leopard.

Chapter II

The Federal System

Federal and Unitary Systems

IN EVERY country there are local or district units of government. There is, therefore, some decentralization of political authority. In a federal system this element of decentralization is frozen into the fundamental law of the land. Between the national government on the one hand and the local units on the other, the powers of government are parceled by the constitution. Formal changes in this division can be made only by amending the highest law. This is the pith of federalism. In the United States, for example, the powers of the national government are written in the national constitution. All other powers are reserved to the states. No alteration can be made in the letter of this division except by amending the constitution. Ours, therefore, is a federal system. What specific powers are given over to the national government we shall have occasion to learn as in one connection or another the more important of these powers are later referred to.

THE FEDERAL SYSTEM

In contrast stands the centralized or unitary system. The powers of the local units are written in ordinary statutes. The central government has complete legal power to contract, withdraw, or in any wise modify these powers at pleasure. In England, for example, boroughs and counties enjoy their powers wholly at the sufferance of Parliament. The same thing is true of the local units in France; they derive no powers whatever from the fundamental laws of the nation.

A basic assumption of federalism is a written constitution. For it is difficult to see how a truly federal system could grow out of the soil of mere custom. But conversely federalism is not a basic assumption of a written constitution. Many countries with written constitutions have no federal element in their governments.

As we have seen, our national constitution may be formally amended only by the joint action of both Congress and the states. The written words, therefore, by which our federal division of powers is made cannot be altered at the will of the national government alone. Three fourths of the states must consent. The British self-governing dominions—Canada, Australia, South Africa—are also organized on the federal plan. In legal view their

Consent of States

constitutions are mere statutes of the Imperial Parliament. But they are statutes, let it be said, in respect to which, reluctantly or otherwise, the legally omnipotent Parliament in London takes orders from overseas. In practise the Canadian parliament has asked only for changes to which the provinces have also consented. In Australia and South Africa the commonwealth itself may alter the imperial statute which is its constitution. In the former the states share in this amending process. In the latter they do not participate.

Since the tendency under most federal systems is inveterately toward centralization, the participation of the states in making amendments is an important element in the preservation of the federal idea. But it is not an element of all so-called federal systems. The constitutions of Germany and Austria, for example, may be amended by action of the central government alone. In consequence the states as such have little or no "protection" even in the paltry powers that have been left to them. They are in a position of legal helplessness almost identical with that of English counties and boroughs. This is federalism in thinnest guise.

Is the distinction between a federal and a unitary system of government based upon a legalistic

THE FEDERAL SYSTEM

or a realistic concept of politics? It is easy to say that Parliament can legally destroy all powers of local government in England; but practically Parliament can do nothing of the kind. Such action would not be tolerated. It is easy to say that our national government cannot without the approval of three-fourths of the states enlarge its powers at the expense of state powers. But the fact is that to some extent the national government can and does do this, as we shall see, even though without the consent of the states it cannot change the actual wording of the constitution.

We speak of our national government as one of limited powers. We say that it is limited to the powers expressly or impliedly granted by the constitution. This is, however, half truth, half fiction. True the words of the constitution appear to confer only specific powers. But look the situation squarely in the face. Written words have no binding force except as they are given such force by human interpretations and applications. Under every written constitution some organ or organs of the government itself have the power to determine the measure of the government's own competence. The government decides for itself what the words of the constitution imply and how far it may go in

Limited or Unlimited Powers

[37]

THE LIVING CONSTITUTION

the exercise of powers. The government of the United States is no exception. In most countries this power of self-determination, of self-expansion, of self-aggression, resides in the national legislature. With us this power is initially in Congress and ultimately in the courts, especially in the Supreme Court. But the Supreme Court is merely an organ of the government. It is none the less so because of the high esteem in which it is commonly held or because of its general aloofness from partisan politics. Whatever is enacted by Congress and approved by the Supreme Court is valid even though to the rest of us it is in plain violation of an unmistakable fiat of the fundamental law. "Things may be legal and yet unconstitutional," Lord Brougham once said of English law. The paradox is equally true of American law. There is no limitation imposed upon the national government which Congress, the President, and the Supreme Court, acting in consecutive agreement, may not legally override. In this sense the government as a whole is clearly a government of unlimited powers; for by interpretation it stakes out its own boundaries.

Take a concrete example. The national constitution vests no power in Congress to establish and

THE FEDERAL SYSTEM

maintain public education. But the constitution does vest power to establish and maintain an army and a navy. Suppose that Congress, taking the absurd view that an army and a navy could be adequately recruited only by setting up complete control of elementary and secondary education, should provide by law for a system of national public education. And suppose the Supreme Court upheld this law. Such an exercise of power by the government could not be further questioned, however violent the twist of the constitution by which it was sustained. With one fell swoop the power of the states to control education would disappear; for children could not be coincidentally educated in two sets of schools.

This, then, is the situation that results from the power of the government (including the Supreme Court) to fix by interpretation the measure of its own constitutional competence. What the national government elects to do it may legally do. From this point of view the difference between a federal system and a centralized system of government is, like the difference between a written and an unwritten or a flexible and a rigid constitution, a difference only of degree. But in practical operation, again, the difference is by no means trivial. There

THE LIVING CONSTITUTION

are limits to the flexibility even of flexible words. The Supreme Court does not covet self-stultification. Moreover Congressmen and Senators come from the states, and the people of the states would not stand idly by and witness the wholesale filching of state powers by a highhanded Congress aided and abetted by a pliant court. It would be wellnigh inconceivable that Congress could, by process of expansion, gradually draw unto itself all political powers and thus destroy the federal system branch and root. Federalism in the United States is not a fiction; it is a vital reality. The concept is both legalistic and factual. Nor is it vanishing or even weakening in any marked degree, despite the prevailing notion to the contrary.

National Invasion of State Powers

It has become the mode in recent years to look upon every novel use of the powers of Congress as an encroachment upon the powers reserved to the states, as an infraction of the federal division made by the constitution. National expansion of power there has been, and upon a vast scale. But there has been far less resulting contraction of state powers than is commonly credited. In point of fact the powers of both units of government have greatly enlarged in exercise. There has been deafening hue and cry over a few matters; but

THE FEDERAL SYSTEM

viewed in the large no very substantial deflation of state powers is traceable to federal inflation.

The prevalent misconception in respect to this matter derives from two sources. In the first place there has been an amount of "interference" with state powers by the federal courts. But this "encroachment" comes not from Congress; it comes from the judiciary. For instance, this or that scheme of state taxation is held to obstruct interstate commerce. Or this or that program of social legislation or method of public utility control by the states is held to deprive persons of liberty or property without due process of law. The states are thus held submissive to the courts' views of the meaning of certain vague phrases of the constitution. But this has, in many if not most instances, nothing whatever to do with the constitutional division of powers between the nation and the states. The fact that the states may not constitutionally exercise this or that power does not necessarily signify that Congress may exercise such power. But many persons, seeing the powers of the states thus invaded, do not pause to distinguish between judicial and congressional invasion.

In the second and far more important place, the actual effect of an exercise of power by Congress

[41]

Commerce Power is, in its relation to the exercise of corresponding power by the states, often misapprehended. Congress has augmented the exercise of national powers chiefly under its constitutional grant of power "to regulate commerce with foreign nations and among the several states". Now both "regulate" and "commerce" are words that are fruitful of power; and in latter years Congress has recognized the power of these words to generate power in Congress. In the early days, before commerce had ruthlessly repudiated the boundaries of states, the courts groped somewhat uncertainly but none the less warily for meanings and applications of these words. On the whole they displayed remarkably happy foresight in the matter. However that may be, it was ultimately held generally that the power in Congress to regulate interstate and foreign commerce must be construed to inhibit the states from doing to such commerce anything that amounted to "regulation". It was settled that the states could not regulate interstate or foreign commerce whether Congress had done so or not. Except for congressional regulation, such commerce was to be "free and untrammeled". If the field of regulation was to be occupied at all, it must be occupied by Congress.

THE FEDERAL SYSTEM

This sounds very simple. It seems to mark an easily discerned boundary between the exerted or potential powers of Congress and a complete lack of power in the states. It appears to say that when Congress marches into some hitherto unoccupied field of commerce regulation, it does not drive the states out; it merely pitches tent in one of its own waste places. Sometimes this is true; sometimes it is not. The apparent simplicity is in fact the height of complexity. Let us illustrate.

However busy Congress has been in recent years in occupying directly or indirectly the field of regulating interstate and foreign commerce, it made haste in this matter very slowly. Apart from navigation, immigration, and tariff laws (which latter laws could also be referred to its power to lay imposts and duties), Congress did nothing of importance toward regulating commerce by law until in 1887 it created the Interstate Commerce Commission. Did this law and the numerous laws by which the powers of this Commission have since been strengthened and increased infringe upon the powers of the states? Yes and no.

Prior to this action by Congress the states had attempted in more or less bungling fashion to regulate railroads in the interest of securing adequate

[43]

THE LIVING CONSTITUTION

and non-discriminatory service at reasonable rates.
Impotence of States
The courts sustained the power of the state governments to subject public utilities of this kind to control; but again and again they declared that this or that kind of regulation by the states was void because it interfered with the free flow of commerce between the states.

What other ruling was possible? Of all the enterprises in the country railroads were the primary enterprises engaged in commerce. By consolidations of originally short lines their business was daily becoming more and more interstate in character. At many points of needed control the states were, and properly were, powerless. Chiefly for this reason Congress created the Interstate Commerce Commission. It was to exercise power which, under judicial interpretation of the constitution, the states could not exercise and which they certainly should not have been able to exercise in all common sense. On crossing into a state that sought to outlaw discriminations, a railroad company could not very easily give back a just proportion of the unjust rebate it had left to a large shipper in a less exacting state of departure. It could not very easily inform the small or unfavored shipper that the interstate train was now passing into

[44]

an unregenerate state where his goods would have to pay a higher rate. It could not, if it hoped to capitalize on its reason for giving the pass, awake an important politician in the middle of the night to tell him that the efficacy of his free travel certificate had run out at the boundary of a state that prohibited passes. It could not at a state line alter its accounting system, or the form of its bills of lading, or the amount of its watered stock, any more than it could change the character of its brakes, or the length of its caboose cars, or the color of its engineers' hair. There are many things that the states could not regulate because in attempting to do so they would have seriously interfered with interstate commerce whether Congress had acted or not. To this extent—and it is a very large extent—Congress did not, in creating and extending the powers of the Interstate Commerce Commission, encroach upon the powers of the states. Today the powers of the national Commission over railroads utterly dwarf the powers of the state commissions. But in large part this is the logic of facts rather than of law. The interstate business of railroads and allied carriers is far greater than their intra-state business. Moreover, in many aspects it is impossible to separate the one from the other for purposes of regulation. The two are inextricably intermingled.

Encroach-ment on States

For this last mentioned reason, if for no other, it would be false to say that the exertion of national control over interstate commerce through the medium of the Interstate Commerce Commission has not invaded the powers of the states. In theory each state still enjoys full power to regulate the business of railroads within its boundaries. In practise this power is limited by the mere fact of national regulation of interstate business. For example, the national commission prescribes a system of accounting or a uniform bill of lading for interstate business. Almost of necessity these must be adopted by the states for intra-state business. But if there were no national prescription in these matters it is highly probable that the states could and would regulate such matters as to intra-state business, however unsatisfactory the net result of varying state regulations might be. Moreover it is highly probable that the courts would sustain many such state regulations even though they incidentally affected interstate commerce. Or take as another example the case of a state rate that is held void because it discriminates against an interstate rate established by the railroads and approved

THE FEDERAL SYSTEM

as reasonable by the national Commission. If there were no national rate it is most unlikely that the courts would declare the state rate void simply because it discriminated against an interstate rate fixed by the railroads themselves.

In other words, where Congress has acted positively upon interstate commerce, the negation upon the powers of the states is larger and more effective than it is when Congress merely fails to act. It is one thing to declare the action of a state void because it collides with an express mandate of the national Commission as to interstate commerce. It is quite a different thing to declare such action void because it interferes generally with a latent and unexercised power of Congress to regulate interstate commerce. Had the Interstate Commerce Commission never been established there is no doubt whatever that the powers of state commissions today would be very much more extensive than they are in fact.

More than this, the courts have been by no means consistent in their application of the rule that commerce, in the absence of congressional action, must not be regulated by the states. Take workmen's compensation laws. The national Employers' Liability Act and the workmen's com-

Inconsis-[tencies

[47]

pensation laws of the various states were enacted at about the same time—in the decade from 1905 to 1915. The former applied only to railroads engaged in interstate and foreign commerce. It was, after amendment, sustained as valid regulation of interstate commerce. It was held to be a safety regulation though manifestly it was in fact a measure enacted in the interest of economic equity. The Court also declared that as to railroad employees engaged in interstate commerce the national law and not the laws of the state must be applied. But the Court did not intimate that had there been no national law the state laws would have been inapplicable to this class of employees. Quite the contrary was the intimation. Yet if the national law was a regulation of interstate commerce, then by the same token so were the state laws in their application to these interstate employees. Logic and consistency would have required that they be held void as to such application whether there were any national law or not.

Or take as another example the safety appliances laws governing railroad equipment. The national laws upon this subject are held to brush aside the state laws wherever there is actual conflict; but unless there is conflict most of these state

THE FEDERAL SYSTEM

laws are valid even though they apply to interstate commerce. The same is true of quarantine laws against human, animal, or plant diseases.

Despite the general rule of freedom of commerce, therefore, it is manifest that when Congress undertakes to regulate interstate commerce specifically, it does to some extent take over powers which, in the absence of such regulation, are permitted to the states under judicial interpretation of the constitution. It is not merely occupying an unoccupied field of control.

It is important also to consider as bearing upon our federal division of powers the effect upon state powers of a wholly different class of laws which Congress has, with the sanction of the courts, enacted under the guise of regulating interstate and foreign commerce. These are in fact police power enactments. Their aim is to promote public morals or health or safety rather than to promote or control commerce. Here again it is necessary to revert to the rule of freedom of commerce. If commerce among the states is to be free from state control needless to say no state can at will prohibit the importation into its borders of goods from another state. Moreover the Supreme Court early laid down the well known rule that the

National Police Powers

right to import carries with it the right to sell, at least in the "original package"—that is, the package before it has been broken and the goods in consequence have become "mixed" with other goods in the state, usually for purposes of retail sale.

Now the power to enact laws in the interest of such matters as the public morals, health, and safety—in short, the police power—belongs primarily to the states. But in the exercise of this power, in imposing prohibitions of one sort or another, the states sometimes found that their laws were partly if not largely nullified by the federal right of their residents to import and sell in the original package. How could a state in such circumstances enforce a law prohibiting the sale of intoxicating liquors? It could not do so. More than this, the adequate enforcement of some laws required supervision and control of the source of supply of commodities. How could the state of New York prohibit the sale of canned meats which had been packed under unsanitary conditions in Chicago or Omaha? It could not do so. In a number of instances, therefore, Congress came to the rescue with the cudgel of interstate commerce. In some instances it carried the rescue much further than many of the states desired. It is only by a spe-

THE FEDERAL SYSTEM

cific examination of these laws that one can assess their effect upon the powers of the states.

Congress has excluded from interstate commerce lottery tickets and obscene literature and pictures. Punishment is imposed on the shipper. Now all of the states prohibit the sale of these. The national laws, therefore, merely aid the states. They provide an additional, not a substitute, penalty. Congress has by similar law excluded birth control devices and information. As to these matters the laws of the states vary. To the extent that the sale of such devices or the dissemination of such information is not prohibited by either the state in which the shipment is made or the state in which it is received, it seems clear that Congress has invaded the powers of the states. It has affected their internal policies. And this was the deliberate and exclusive purpose of the law. For people do not ship for the pleasure of shipping; and manifestly contraceptive devices and information can do no harm in transit. Precisely the same may be said of the law which barred the doors of interstate commerce to prize fight films.

Examples of Police Power Laws

Congress has prohibited the transportation in interstate commerce of women and girls for immoral purposes. The laws of all the states prohibit prostitution; but they differ in the matter of imposing punishment for sexual immorality of a non-commercial character. Moreover, one and all of the states are lax in the enforcement of such laws. To the extent that the national law goes beyond the laws of a particular state, it certainly appears to encroach upon the power of the state when it, in effect though not in terms, provides punishment in that state for an act that is legally innocent under the state laws.

Congress has also closed interstate commerce to adulterated and misbranded foods and drugs. All of the states have pure food and drug laws; and although they are probably in no instance identical with the national law and the regulations issued thereunder, the act of Congress may properly be regarded as a valuable supplement to and not a substitute for the state laws. Certain it is that state and local activity in the enforcement of such laws has vastly increased rather than diminished since the enactment of the federal law in 1906. The Meat Inspection Act of the same year placed the big packers of the Middle West under government supervision and control which none of the many states into which their products are shipped had the power to apply.

THE FEDERAL SYSTEM

The Webb-Kenyon Act of 1913 prohibited the shipment in interstate commerce of intoxicating liquors "intended by any persons interested therein, to be received, possessed, sold, or in any manner used" in violation of the law of the state of their destination. Clearly in this act Congress was merely wielding the weapon of interstate commerce in aid of the prohibition states. Far from drawing unto itself any power of the states it was in effect allowing the states to draw unto themselves a power of the federal government. But the Reed "Bone-Dry" Amendment of 1917 was of another color. Without interfering with the freedom of the "wet" states, it made the prohibition states more prohibitory than they had elected to be. Where a limited amount of liquor was allowed by the state to be imported for personal consumption, the Reed Amendment prohibited this. In sustaining the law the Supreme Court said in explanation that while Congress might use its power over interstate commerce "in aid of the policy of the state, if it wishes to do so, it is equally clear that the policy of Congress acting independently may induce legislation without reference to the particular policy or law of any given state". As a general proposition this is true enough. But what a strangely inequitable re-

Liquor Laws

sult. The wet states, the local option states, could have their way unfettered. But the near-dry states were to be made by act of Congress completely arid deserts. Dissenting, Mr. Justice McReynolds called this "direct intermeddling with the states' internal affairs". And in the inequality of its operation, such it unquestionably was. With greater propriety Congress might have prohibited all shipment of liquor in interstate commerce, although this would certainly have affected the internal policies of the wet states. But to single out the prohibition states for more stringent prohibition than they desired was, to put it mildly, a unique example of congressional unreasonableness—one might almost say impudence. The Webb-Kenyon Act is perhaps our best illustration of the exercise of Congressional power in aid of state power; and the Reed Amendment to that act is perhaps our worst example of the exercise of congressional power in restraint of legitimate state powers.

Summary of Effects From this cursory review of some of the more important laws enacted by Congress under its power to regulate interstate and foreign commerce, we may conclude as follows: To a considerable extent these laws do not trespass upon the powers of the states; they occupy a field of control from which

THE FEDERAL SYSTEM

the states are ousted by the naked grant of the commerce power to Congress. To a considerable extent also they merely supplement the laws of the states without in any manner supplanting them. This is especially true when the law of Congress applies a policy that conforms in substance to state policies that are practically uniform throughout the country. In a few instances these national laws do nothing more than bring federal aid to the states in making their own state policies more effective. On the other hand, to some extent they do operate to withdraw powers from the states; they occupy a field fringes of which—and sometimes more than fringes—have hitherto been occupied by the states; and by positive national occupation they preclude further possible invasion of the field by the states. Moreover, in some instances the sole intent of these laws is to make the execution of some internal social policy of the state difficult if not impossible. This is particularly true when the law of Congress deals with a subject in respect to which the states have widely varying policies.

The situation is complicated. There is no use glossing the fact. To simplify would be to falsify. Out of the legal confusion, however, and the welter of words in which it is compassed, there emerges the fact that the federal division of powers between the nation and the states is, in variable measure, subject to alteration by act of Congress. The national axe has been laid to some of the limbs of state powers and will without doubt be laid to others. But it has not been laid to the roots. And in spite of the pruning the tree grows and flourishes. It should be said, moreover, that in addition to the implement of the commerce clause Congress has available for this purpose the less efficacious tools of the taxing and the postal powers.

Services-in-aid

Mention should be made here also of the numerous services which have been established by Congress in fields that lie for the most part beyond the range of its regulatory powers. These are investigational, informational, advisory, even hortatory. For the advancement of the interests of agriculture, education, road-building, mining, manufacturing, commerce, labor, public health, a large number of these promotional services have been set up. For example, Congress cannot regulate labor within a state, but it maintains a Department of Labor which collects and publishes a large amount of information and generally promotes the interests of labor. Such services swell the budget of the nation appreciably. They expand its adminis-

THE FEDERAL SYSTEM

trative organization far beyond what the powers enumerated in the constitution would seem to imply. But even where these services bear relations to state powers and services they do not actually trespass upon them. Yet collectively they carry the national government direct to the people over the heads of the states. They exalt its relative importance. They seemingly magnify its powers.

A few of these services take the form of grants of money to the states in aid of certain public enterprises. Military, agricultural, and vocational education are all subsidized by the national government. So is the building of roads. There are grants in aid for mothers' pensions. And there is constant pressure upon Congress to extend grants to the states for other purposes. Now it may seem paradoxical to speak of a bounty as an encroachment. But money talks—no less in nation-state relations than in other human relations. It beckons and lures even where there is a string attached. And every national gift to the states is dangled upon a string. If they accept they must conform to the national requirements, whatever they may be. To this extent their internal policies are of necessity affected. In theory they yield voluntarily; in practise they have little choice. As yet the system

Grants-in-aid

of grants-in-aid has not been widely applied. It has not seriously modified the federal division. But there is nothing obscure about the transforming potentiality of the system.

Federalism and Nationalism

Most federal systems in the world originated in hard political facts. They were not born of abstraction. It would have been impossible in 1789 to fuse the American states into a completely centralized union. The most difficult task of the advocates of the constitution was to convince its opponents that the degree of centralization for which it provided was not an unmitigated evil. British and French Canada could not have been brought together in anything closer than a federal system in 1867. Historic and dynastic influences prevented the formation of a unitary government in the German Empire in 1866-71. The Australian and South African federal systems were likewise founded on political expediency.

But political facts change. The stupendous growth of nationalism in the latter nineteenth and early twentieth centuries was an almost universal phenomenon throughout the world. And nationalism is innately the foe of federalism. The two are antithetical. Before the waxing spirit of nationalism, it was inevitable that the jealousies and

THE FEDERAL SYSTEM

rivalries, the self-love and self-sufficiency, of local units should in some measure wane.

Nor is this the whole story. Apart from the mental attitude that is implicit in the term nationalism, the economic life of every industrial country has been and is being nationalized upon a tremendous and ever widening scale. In the United States transportation, communication, the consolidation and expansion of business enterprise, the concentration of capital, the organization of labor, have all developed in almost complete disregard of state lines. Economically we have become largely integrated, unified, sectionally interdependent. This is indisputable fact.

Over against this economic synthesis, however, we maintain our political decentralization—our federalism. Few if any of our states have elements of natural economic or geographic unity. Their lines are at best historical accidents; at worst geodetic irrelevancies. But the states are not, as Metternich once sneered of Italy, mere "geographical expressions". They are very real and very powerful political and legal entities. Over our integrated national economy they exercise a disintegrated control. A corporation that is engaged in nation-wide business is the creation of some particular

THE LIVING CONSTITUTION

state and is "admitted" to do business in the other states. It is taxed by each of the states, often upon different principles. What it may or must do in one state it may not always or need not always do in another. The transportation systems of the country, although subject to national control in considerable part, are also subject to no little state control and especially to varying kinds of state taxation. A national labor organization finds itself in one situation under the laws of this state and perhaps in an altogether different situation under the laws of some other state.

Of course it is possible to overdraw this picture. There is, when all is said, a deal of similarity in the laws of the several states. But there is also a deal of dissimilarity. And in any case, regulation by the states instead of by some central authority means a prodigious increase in the number of public authorities with which private economic enterprises must have relations. On the face of things the system seems to produce needless trouble.

Reasons for Federal-[ism

Why then do we tolerate this disharmony between our economic and our political organizations? Why not scrap our federalism? In answer one may allege the tradition that clings to every hoary institution—and certainly among the polit-

[60]

ical systems of the world ours may now be counted hoary. There is likewise the inevitable, and no doubt salutary, inertia to radical and fundamental change that permeates the body of every stable political system. But there are reasons other than these why we cling to our federalism.

This is a vast and diversified country. A division of powers which leaves to the states a large and important sphere of autonomy, whatever its disadvantages, has at least one obvious advantage that is of great importance. It offers the opportunity for economic and political experimentation under the urge of a local opinion that does not have to wait to convert the entire nation to its hopes and its beliefs.

We are told that men are imitative animals. So are states. Politico-economic experiments, proved and unproved, improved and unimproved, spread contagiously from state to state. For the states are notorious copyists. One might almost speak with propriety of their "herd instinct". Moreover, even in matters upon which Congress ultimately takes federal action the states usually point the way. State control of railroads preceded that of Congress. State action prohibiting the sale of liquor preceded the eighteenth amendment.

Many states extended suffrage to women before the nineteenth amendment. The executive budget system in the states foreran the half-way measure of Congress. The states tackled the problem of industrial accidents long before Congress did, and workmen's compensation laws were enacted in some of the states before the national law was passed. State minimum wage laws antedated the law which Congress applied to the District of Columbia, though all such laws were struck down by the Supreme Court. Adequate child labor laws prevailed in many states prior to the abortive attempts at congressional regulation or the proposal of the constitutional amendment which was rejected by the states.

And disregardful of state action upon subjects that are also within the purview of Congress, there are subjects of exclusive state action upon which it is unlikely that Congress would have acted had all the powers of government been concentrated in Washington. Would home rule for cities be known? Would the initiative, referendum, and recall have been heard of? Control over local public utilities is sufficiently unsatisfactory under state regulation; it would be almost unthinkable under national regulation.

THE FEDERAL SYSTEM

We may approve or disapprove of any or all of these policies. That is beside the point. They are at any rate among the more important policies that have made politics in recent years. And in practically every instance it is the states that have taken the initiative. Congress has trailed behind them.

It may be urged that had there been no states Congress would have acted more promptly on many of these subjects. This can neither be affirmed nor denied. It is a matter of conjecture. But most intelligent observers would probably hazard an emphatic denial.

Another advantage of the federal system is that the states are reservoirs from which national leadership may be drawn. Many who are elected to the national legislature or appointed to federal office have served apprenticeships in the states. Moreover, for reasons to be mentioned later, our national government seems peculiarly ill-organized for the development of nation-wide leadership pointing to the highest office of leadership in the land, the presidency. Of a truth not all of our Presidents are leaders in any true sense either before or after taking office. But the office postulates leadership, and sometimes the facts are in accord. Of its eleven incumbents since Grant, six, including

Cleveland, Roosevelt, and Wilson, were drafted from the governorships of the states. Only three, Garfield, Harrison, and Harding, came from the Senate; only one, Taft, from the Cabinet.

Still another advantage of the federal system is that it avoids the danger of a colossal and ubiquitous bureaucracy centering in and emanating from Washington. This is not to assume that, with the destruction of federalism, Congress would provide no local self-government. Inevitably it would be compelled to do so. But it is to assume, and with justifiable warrant, that centralized administration would be enormously increased. The very thought of the possibilities and probabilities that inhere in this should be sufficient to give pause to the purblind or heedless advocate of centralization.

These then are some of the advantages of federalism in a country of the giant proportions and the economic and social diversities of the United States. No one would be foolish enough to contend that the people have rationalized them in the fashion herein attempted. They merely see the system in fairly successful operation. They merely enjoy its advantages without much if any conscious reflection or philosophising. Especially do they enjoy the opportunity for local "trial and error"

THE FEDERAL SYSTEM

within the sphere of state autonomy. This is probably why our federalism has been saved from the scrap-heap of institutional discards.

One other point is worth recording. We study our constitutional system largely from the cases that have been decided by the courts. These disclose the difficulties which the system entails. They emphasize chiefly conflicts of jurisdiction and of power. We are wont in consequence to regard the system as one that is productive principally of troubles. We come to think of it as consisting wholly of an intricate maze of delicate and fine-spun adjustments. But in focusing attention so sharply upon the difficulties we become near-sighted. We fail to see the fairly smooth working of the system as a whole. It is not the weak, the lumbering, the perverse, the transitory, the unworkable, thing that its detractors assert it to be. Moreover, at innumerable points where clashes of authority between the central and the state governments would be conceivable there is in practise a large amount of harmonious cooperation between them.

We commonly associate the doctrine of states' rights with the nullifiers and secessionists of the South. This is because it was argued to its conclusion with superfine logic by a South Carolinian, Calhoun, and was put to the supreme test by secession and war. But the truth is that the doctrine knows no special sectional habitation. It is a nomad, reviving whenever and dwelling wherever toes are trod upon or feelings severely ruffled by the exercise of federal power. From the Virginia and Kentucky Resolutions of 1798 to the prohibition amendment of 1919 every such exercise that has met with substantial popular disapproval has been denounced by its opponents, wherever resident, as an interference with the "rights" of the states. In a country such as ours, where questions of constitutionality are the talk of dinner tables, this is natural even though sometimes nonsensical.

States' Rights

The prohibition amendment is the latest subject of bitter debate. Upon an almost absurdly exaggerated theory of states' rights the Supreme Court was actually asked to declare this duly adopted amendment void. As if the states enjoy certain inherent powers from nature or from God—powers which they are impotent to transfer to the national government even by unanimous consent of the governed. One may approve or disapprove of the policy of prohibition or of the policy of writing it in drastic words of compulsion into the fun-

THE FEDERAL SYSTEM

damental law of the nation. One may be firmly convinced that control over the sale of intoxicating liquors should be a state right as a matter of policy. But "states' rights" is a term of law, not of policy. Legally and voluntarily the states, acting by their legislatures, surrendered this legal right to the nation. Let people continue at will to discuss recapturing the right, or modifying the enforcement law, or allowing the amendment to atrophy; but in the name of reason let all discussion of states' rights in this connection cease.

The confusion in respect to states' rights is attributable largely to the fact just mentioned, that historically and properly the term refers to the legal rather than the befitting rights of the states. Mr. Dicey, like many other commentators on federalism, cavalierly strikes off the appropriate division of powers between the nation and the states by saying: "The details of this division vary under every different federal constitution, but the general principle on which it should rest is obvious. Whatever concerns the nation as a whole should be placed under control of the national government. All matters which are not primarily of common interest should remain in the hands of the several states."

Problem of Federal Division

THE LIVING CONSTITUTION

The fault with this principle, as with many "general principles", is that it is palsied and infirm of its own generality. Furthermore, even if its practicality be conceded, it is of highly doubtful value. There never was a system embodying a substantial degree of federalism in which the states were deprived of control over all matters that might reasonably be said to concern the nation as a whole. In respect to a very few subjects there can be no argument. It goes without saying that the national government must of necessity control foreign affairs; and this embraces a good many incidents. It must wage war and make peace. To this end it must have some, though not necessarily complete, control over military affairs. It must have financial powers exigent to its needs. Perhaps coinage, standards of weights and measures, patents, and copyrights are also essentially subjects of national direction, although state regulation of these, however annoying and absurd, would not be inconceivable. But at or near this point the list of indispensables ends, and the problem of the federal division begins.

Consider some of the powers that are given to our national government. It operates the postal service; but this is no more inherently a national

THE FEDERAL SYSTEM

function than is the maintenance of the railway, express, telephone, and telegraph services. It has power to regulate interstate commerce. No doubt it would be necessary to prohibit the states from seriously interfering with or obstructing such commerce, although as we have seen the constitution did not oust the states from this field in so many words. No doubt also it is highly desirable, in view of the nationalization of commerce in fact, that Congress should have power to subject such commerce to a measure of uniform control. It should not be forgotten, however, that, possessing this power from the beginning, Congress used it scarcely at all during the first century of the existence of the federal division. Control over bankruptcies, which is vested in Congress, concerns the entire nation no more than control over any number of other business relations that are now and always have been regulated by the states.

It is, however, especially in the realm of the powers that are reserved to the American states—in the sacrosanct region of states' rights—that opinions differ and will probably always differ as to what is a matter "primarily of common interest". Is public education such a matter? Is the regulation of marriage and divorce? National suffrage and national elections? Crime prevention and criminal punishment? The creation and control of corporations doing business in many states? Labor conditions in all of their manifold regulatory aspects? Banking and insurance? The entire body of law governing civil and commercial relations? The law of real and personal property? The law of inheritance?

To put such questions as these is to state the real problem of the federal division. In relatively minor degree is it a matter of applying an obvious general principle. Concededly a very few powers must indispensably be vested in the central government. But this is almost child's play. The knots of an adult problem remain. And contrary to widespread popular notion the problem is far more largely that of preserving vitality in the states than of adequately equipping the national government to go forth to war upon the sins of state omission and commission. If federalism is to be a reality, the states must have real powers; and this means that they must have control over numerous matters that are from many points of view of nation-wide interest and importance. If every power for which the "common interest" argument can be cogently put forward were to be transferred to the national

THE FEDERAL SYSTEM

government, federalism would give up the ghost, as it has given it up in all but name in Germany and Austria. If it is to live, there must be in its make-up a large amount of the artificial, the arbitrary, the illogical, the unscientific.

Indeed, under any genuinely federal system one might almost say of states' rights that "whatever is is right".

Chapter III

Bills of Rights

THE point has been made that, considered in its totality, our national government is one of unlimited powers since it has authority to rate its own constitutional competence. But the point was made in the same connection that in another sense it is very properly regarded as a limited government. For its powers are reduced to words; and there are limits in reason as well as in politics to the extravagant meanings that may be wrung from words. And of course it was never intended for a moment to intimate that Congress is a legally omnipotent legislature. On the contrary its acts are subject to the suspending veto of the President and to the sustaining veto of the courts.

The prime restriction upon the national government is that its powers are recited in the constitution one by one. It cannot, except as the courts consent, go beyond the implications of the list that is thus prescribed to it. All other powers belong to the states. But in addition to this the constitution

BILLS OF RIGHTS

imposes upon the national government and especially upon Congress a series of positive prohibitions. In a number of matters it also affirmatively constrains the states. A few of these inhibitions are in identical terms riveted upon both the national and the state governments.

Most of these prohibitory clauses of the national constitution appear to supply the individual with defensive armament against the government. Commonly they are lumped together and called a "bill of rights". They are said to create a sphere of private rights and immunities which the government may not invade. They are alleged to protect the individual in his rights of person and of property from being thoughtlessly or churlishly shouldered out of the way. Addressed to the government, they are all in the nature of thou-shalt-nots. But these commandments are not uniform in their effects upon individual rights. Where they lay hands of restraint upon the government in its direct relations to the individual, they do indeed equip him with weapons of defense against the government. But where they fetter the power of the government to regulate relations between individual and individual, the net result is quite otherwise. In such event the crowning consequence

What are Bills of Rights?

THE LIVING CONSTITUTION

of these prohibitions is not so much to arm the individual against the government as it is to arm him for the defense of his rights against rights which the government attempts to assert in behalf of other individuals. The arming of one is the disarming of another. The triumph of one right is the defeat of another. Whether in such instances one looks upon these prohibitions as protective or as destructive of rights depends often upon one's self-interest or upon one's agreement or disagreement with the economic or social views of the courts. It is at any rate certainly insufficient to say that our bills of rights do nothing more than create and protect from governmental encroachment a sphere of private rights and immunities. They protect some rights from public impairment and other rights from private impairment sanctioned by the legislature. Let us illustrate.

Private Right vs. Public Power

The bill of rights prohibits the suspension of the privilege of the writ of *habeas corpus*, or the enactment of a bill of attainder or an *ex post facto* law. It defines treason. It declares that "Congress shall make no law respecting an establishment of religion, or prohibiting the free exercise thereof; or abridging the freedom of speech or of the press; or the right of the people peaceably to assemble, and to petition the government for a redress of grievances." It forbids unreasonable searches and seizures; or the taking of private property for public use without just compensation. It guarantees indictment by grand jury and trial by petit jury and otherwise surrounds the person accused of crime with elements of protection against unfairness. It prohibits excessive bail, excessive fines, cruel and unusual punishments.

Now manifestly all of these things concern the direct relations of the government to the individual. They assert his rights over against the government. They intrench and buttress these rights against governmental attack.

But the bill of rights also declares that neither the national government nor the states shall deprive any person of life, liberty, or property without due process of law. Let us look closely at the effects which this spacious guaranty has upon private rights. Does it afford them protection against the power of the government or against the assertion of other private rights by the government? The answer is that, as expounded by the courts, it does both of these things.

The due process clause has been applied chiefly in relation to action by the states. So applied it has been held to include some, but not all, of the more specific private rights mentioned above. Thus it includes the prohibition against the taking of private property for public use without just compensation. In judicial proceedings the individual must be given due notice and the opportunity to be heard before a competent tribunal; but he need not be indicted by grand jury or tried by a petit jury. He does not enjoy protection against self-incrimination; but a penal law must state a sufficiently definite standard of conduct so that the individual may know whether or not he is conforming to its requirements. In the Gitlow case, decided in 1925, we were for the first time told that due process also includes the guaranty of freedom of speech. In matters of state taxation, too, due process imposes restrictions; such as that the state must have jurisdiction over the thing taxed, and the taxpayer must have notice and the opportunity to be heard upon assessments. It is clear, therefore, that the due process clause does set up a sphere of private rights upon which the state governments may not encroach in their direct relations with individuals. But it does more than this, as applied to both state and national governments.

For example, in 1898 Congress prohibited carriers of interstate commerce from seeking to prevent employees from joining labor unions or from discharging or otherwise discriminating against them because of their membership in such unions. In 1903 Kansas enacted a similar law applicable to all employers in the state. Other states had enacted statutes of like purport. These laws the Supreme Court held void on the ground that they deprived the employers of the right to employ and discharge whomever they chose. To interfere with this right, argued the court, was to deprive the employers of liberty and property without due process of law.

Private Rights and Due Process

But is it not obvious that what Congress and the state legislatures here attempted was to legalize a right of the employees—the right not to be harassed or jeopardized in their employment by reason of membership in trade unions; which right in turn lies at the core of the right of collective bargaining? True the nominal and legal conflict before the courts was between the right of the employer under the constitution and the power of the legislature under the constitution. The vital and ultimate clash, however, was between the private right of the employer under the constitution and the private right of the employee under the statute. These laws set up no direct relationship between the government and the employer. They provided no direct encroachment by administrative or judicial officers upon the rights of the employer. Only in a strictly legalistic sense, a mediate sense, an almost fictional sense, may it be said that the due process clause in this instance protected the right of the individual employer from encroachment by the government. It protected that right from being impinged by the rights of employees. If the employer could rejoice in the protection of his sphere of private rights by the constitution, the employee could with equal propriety mourn the invasion of his sphere of private rights by the constitution. To the latter the bill of rights seemed to destroy rather than to protect private rights.

Precisely the same may be said of the minimum wage laws both of Congress and the states; of the New York eight-hour law for bakeries (the much over-worked adverse decision on which may now be regarded as having been overruled); the Washington law which prohibited employment agencies from accepting fees from persons seeking employment; the Arizona law prohibiting injunctions against peaceful picketing; the ordinance of a Kentucky city which attempted to establish separate residential districts for whites and Negroes;

BILLS OF RIGHTS

and the law creating the Kansas court of industrial relations with powers of compulsory arbitration. All of these laws were declared invalid. All of them regulated primarily relations between individuals. They did not in essence fix relations between the government and individuals.

Of course many laws of this kind have been sustained. Among these are workmen's compensation laws; laws regulating hours of labor for women and children, and for men in unhealthful vocations; requiring employers to furnish discharged or quitting workmen with certificates of service; making "store orders" issued in payment of wages redeemable in cash; compelling mine operators to pay for the mining of coal by weight before screening; directing railway companies to pay wages semi-monthly; requiring such companies to furnish separate accommodations for white and colored persons; prohibiting landlords during a housing shortage from evicting tenants or raising rents. But even where such laws are upheld the contest that is staged in the courts is between private rights that are asserted under the constitution and private rights that are asserted under the statutes. That the latter are held to prevail does not alter the nature of the combat.

THE LIVING CONSTITUTION

Private Rights under Contract Clause

Illustration may also be drawn from the clause of the bill of rights which prohibits the states from passing any law impairing the obligation of contracts. Now most of the contracts which have been alleged or held to be impaired by subsequent state legislation have in theory or in fact been contracts between the state itself (or one of its subdivisions) as one party and an individual (natural person or corporation) as the other party. As applied to such engagements the contract clause clearly establishes protection for the rights of the individual in his direct relations with the government of the state. But the contract clause does not expire with this. It applies also to contracts between individuals. One of its earliest applications was to a bankruptcy law of New York which was held void because it too greatly benefited debtors at the expense of their creditors. It has been held to affect laws governing the conveyance of land from one individual to another, the relations between insurance companies and policy holders, the liability of the stockholders of a corporation to the creditors of the corporation, the rights of mortgagee and of mortgagor, of landlord and tenant, of debtor and creditor generally. To the extent that the contract clause has been declared to affect covenants of this nature it

BILLS OF RIGHTS

has manifestly been employed as a buffer between the contending rights of individuals. True the legal contest has been between the general prescription of the national constitution and the specific prescription of the state law. But the struggle has in fact been the assertion of one private right against another.

To say, then, that our bills of rights offer protection to the individual only against the government is to put entire emphasis on the legalism involved. It is to ignore actualities. It is to imply that the items in the bill of rights operate exclusively to pit private rights against public power. It is to mask the fact that in ultimate effect they often result merely in opposing private right to private right. It is to utter a half-truth or, perhaps more accurately, one aspect of the truth.

Prescriptions in respect to treason, the writ of *habeas corpus*, bills of attainder, *ex post facto* laws, and jury trial were contained in the constitution as it came from the hands of its framers in 1787. The other articles in the bill of rights are found in the first eight amendments, proposed by Congress in 1789 at the behest of the ratifying states. The Federalists protested at the time. Such limitations were unnecessary, they urged, since the

Need for Bill of Rights

national government was one of specifically enumerated powers only. Such a view in 1789 was plausible; but that it should be revoiced, as it is, by certain modern commentators on the constitution appears almost incredible. To regard most of the provisions of these amendments as unnecessary seems to reveal a complete ignorance not only of the political and judicial history of the several articles but also of the distinction between substantive and adjective powers. Have these expositors never heard of the Sedition Act of 1798 or the Espionage Act of 1917? Had the guaranty of freedom of speech no relation to these? Has the protection against unreasonable searches and seizures played no part in the enforcement of internal revenue, smuggling, counterfeiting, postal, liquor prohibition, and numerous other laws enacted under express or implied grant of power? Has the due process clause never been considered in reference to an act of Congress? The government in the exercise of its unmistakable powers must indispensably have power to take private property. Is the requirement of just compensation, then, of no importance? Does the federal government impose no criminal penalties, that the protections afforded to those accused of crime are mere super-

BILLS OF RIGHTS

erogation? And this is not to mention the fact that as to the territories and outlying possessions the national government is one of unenumerated powers. The notion that the specification of federal powers rendered the national bill of rights unnecessary is plainly fantastical.

No adequate comment can here be made upon the history, scope, and significance of the several component parts of the bill of rights. Some of them, such as freedom of religion, the right of assembly and of petition, the right to keep and bear arms, the right not to have soldiers quartered in private houses in time of peace, have, let us hope, passed into the closed book of history. At least this is probably true so far as the danger of national interference is concerned; and these restrictions apply only to the national government. Apart from one or two cases arising out of retaliatory legislation during the Reconstruction era, the guaranties against bills of attainder and *ex post facto* laws have likewise seldom been invoked against Congressional action. As applied to state laws they have been of only occasional importance. A word or two may be appropriately said, however, of a few of the items in the bill of rights that seem of special present-day importance.

THE LIVING CONSTITUTION

Treason and Free Speech

Treason, though a hot and free word upon the tongue in time of national stress, is a cold and well calculated word in the mouth of the constitution. It consists only in "levying war" or in "giving aid and comfort" to the enemy. And there must be an "overt act" of levying or of giving. "Aid and comfort" are, it is true, plastic words; but "overt act" lends itself less readily to passionate distortion. The word treason was frequently bandied during our participation in the World War, not only popularly but also by judges who should have known that it is given a most circumscribed meaning by the constitution. The House of Representatives refused to seat Victor Berger on the ground that he had by publication given aid and comfort to the enemy. But if this were true he should have been convicted of treason, which he was not. In fact scarcely anybody was convicted of treason during the World War, despite the statute of Congress providing punishment for various degrees of this offense. This seems to proclaim an enviable record of liberality. But the proclamation is only apparent. There was little need to invoke the crime of treason. Other criminal statutes were available which did not mention treason.

The restrictions upon punishment for treason

BILLS OF RIGHTS

and upon the abridgment of freedom of speech and the press are seldom of great importance in times of peace. They loom large only in and around times of war and its aftermath. And the most difficult problem presented is that of controlling utterance, whether by word of mouth or in print. For the preservation of the private right of criticism is the heart and soul of the much more important right of public discussion, which in turn is the heart and soul of democracy itself. Now utterance may be an "overt act", as for instance where military secrets are transmitted to the enemy. But most criticisms or denunciations of war aims or war methods or of war *per se* can scarcely be classified as overt acts of treason. Hence it follows that for purposes of controlling utterance the crime of treason, which the constitution has placed in something of a straitjacket, is abandoned. It becomes obsolete. Resort is had to the implied power to punish criminally for any interference or attempted interference with the express power of the government to wage war.

When we entered the World War the government found at hand certain criminal statutes enacted during the Civil War which could be and were used to punish conspiracies to resist recruit-

THE LIVING CONSTITUTION

Espionage Act ing and conscription by riots. And there was quickly made ready a new statute, the Espionage Act, enacted in June, 1917, which applied to individual or casual acts of willful interference with military operations. This act was greatly, although as events proved somewhat belatedly, broadened and stiffened by amendment in May, 1918.

Practically everybody admitted the power of Congress to provide punishment for utterances that actually interfere with military operations. Practically everybody recognized that speech cannot be as free in war as in peace. But the difficulty lay in applying the act to specific utterances. Was this or that utterance, in the particular circumstances involved, made "with intent to interfere with the operation or success of the military or naval forces"? Did it "cause or attempt to cause insubordination"? Did it "willfully obstruct the recruiting or enlistment service"?

The Espionage Act was held valid; but a sharp division arose among judges as to what the Act meant and indeed could mean in view of the constitutional guaranty of freedom of speech. Some of the judges attempted to set up an objective test, like that of Judge Learned Hand: there must be strong danger that the utterance will cause the

BILLS OF RIGHTS

injurious acts sought to be prevented by the statute. Or like that of Mr. Justice Holmes: "The question in every case is whether the words used are used in such circumstances and are of such a nature as to create a clear and present danger that they will bring about the substantive evils that Congress has a right to prevent." On the whole, however, a far broader view of the meaning of the statute and of the competence of Congress to restrict freedom of utterance prevailed.

The whole subject is manifestly fraught with grave difficulties. War entails an abnormal submission to regimentation of conduct. Democracy entails submission to tolerance of discussion. This, if not abnormal, is of a certainty not among the unfailing attributes of human nature. The two are not easily made compatible. Yet sensible compromise must somewhere be struck. At best it is no mere youth's adventure to hold the flaming passions of war in the leash of law. In the heat of conflict the most liberal of statutes may be badly manhandled in application. If err we must, let us err then on the side of liberalism. If hate we must, let us hate without punitive retaliation save where we are certain that retaliation is indispensable. And above all else let the laws restricting freedom of utterance in the blighting winter of war be drafted in the long soft summer of peace. It is only at such time that a reasoned and fairly definitive compromise can be put into competent words. A careful study of the cases actually decided under the Espionage Act would point the way toward a proper statute. But certain it is that, if there must be another war, it should not find the Espionage Act of 1917–18 unamended upon the books.

As has been said, the Supreme Court has finally held that the due process clause includes the guaranty of freedom of speech against state action also. Even more than the Espionage Act do the criminal syndicalism statutes of some of the states need calm reconsideration and sane revision. Mr. Justice Holmes has aptly said that, "With effervescing opinions, as with not yet forgotten champagnes, the quickest way to let them get flat is to let them get exposed to the air." Democracy cannot safely endure laws which attempt to bottle up emotions and stifle opinions.

From what has been said it should not be adduced that the constitutional guaranty of freedom of speech is a rope of sand. Without it we should no doubt have virtually the same discussion of the wisdom or unwisdom of the policy of the govern-

BILLS OF RIGHTS

ment. It is nevertheless salutary to have a constitutional peg upon which the discussion may be hung. Whether this constitutional right was or was not sufficiently vindicated during the last war, freedom of speech was advanced measurably by the mere fact of its wide judicial discussion. In the absence of constitutional provision there would have been far less opportunity—in fact no reason at all—for this discussion by the courts.

The writ of *habeas corpus* is often called the "great writ of liberty". It is perhaps the most famous writ of the law. Certainly it is one of the most important. It is directed by a judge to an official who is holding a person in alleged illegal imprisonment. It demands that the body of the prisoner be brought before the judge that the cause of his detention may be inquired into. There is a good deal that is technical about the precise conditions under which the writ may properly issue. For one thing it is not a writ of review from a higher to a lower court; it is no substitute for a writ of appeal or a writ of error where such writs are accessible. For another thing, except in unusual circumstances, it is employed primarily where lack of jurisdiction is contended rather than where error or injustice is asserted. An example of such unusual

Habeas Corpus

circumstances came before the Supreme Court in 1923. Under mob pressure five Negroes in Arkansas had been hurried to conviction and sentenced to death. Application was made to a federal court for a writ of *habeas corpus*. The Supreme Court said: "The corrective process supplied by the state may be so adequate that interference by *habeas corpus* ought not to be allowed. It certainly is true that mere mistakes of law in the course of a trial are not to be corrected in that way. But if the case is that the whole proceeding is a mask—that counsel, jury and judge were swept to the fatal end by an irresistible wave of public passion, and that the state courts failed to correct the wrong, neither perfection in the machinery for correction nor the possibility that the trial court and counsel saw no other way of avoiding an immediate outbreak of the mob can prevent this court from securing to the petitioners their constitutional right."

On the other hand the notorious Ju Toy case decided in 1905 offers a striking illustration of the failure of the writ of *habeas corpus* to mete justice in circumstances that were not at all unusual. It was there held that the writ should have been denied to a Chinaman seeking entry into the United States because his application alleged nothing ex-

BILLS OF RIGHTS

cept that he was born in this country and was in constitutional consequence a citizen thereof. It was held also that the law could and did make the decision of the immigration authorities on this question of fact final. Reviewing the extraordinary hardships under which the law placed a Chinaman who was required to prove his citizenship at a port of entry distant from his averred place of birth, Mr. Justice Brewer vehemently dissented. "If this," he cried, "is not a star-chamber proceeding of the most stringent sort, what more is necessary to make it one?" The harshness of the Ju Toy decision has been somewhat assuaged in latter years. "It is better," said the Court in 1920, "that many Chinese immigrants should be improperly admitted than that one natural born citizen of the United States should be permanently excluded from his country."

Of course persons seeking admission to the country have seldom had any legal difficulty in securing writs of *habeas corpus* for the review of decisions of immigration officers involving interpretations of the law and not merely questions of fact. Such, for example, was the point raised in 1926 in the widely discussed Cathcart case, where a United States District Court reversed the opinion

THE LIVING CONSTITUTION

of the immigration authorities on the meaning of the statutory phrase "crime of moral turpitude".

Habeas Corpus in War Time

Two famous Civil War cases discussed the power of the government to suspend the writ of *habeas corpus* "when in cases of rebellion or invasion the public safety may require it". The Merryman case, decided in 1861, held that the President, unauthorized by Congress, had no power of suspension. The Milligan case, decided in 1867, held by a bare majority of the court that not even Congress had the power to suspend the writ outside of the theatre of actual military operations. Whatever may be the sound interpretation of the constitution on these points, these decisions were no more than judicial gestures. The prisoners were in the clutches of the military authorities. No civil court could compel their release. These opinions therefore were in the nature of Sermons on the Mount —admonitions to proper constitutional behavior. This fact was pathetically revealed by Chief Justice Taney when he said in concluding his opinion in the Merryman case: "I have exerted all the power which the constitution and laws confer upon me, but that power has been resisted by a force too strong for me to overcome." He issued no order to the military commander. He did all that he

BILLS OF RIGHTS

could do. He filed his opinion and had a copy of it transmitted to the President, respectfully suggesting that he "take care that the laws be faithfully executed" in accordance with the views which had been expressed by the Court.

It thus appears that, whether in peace or in war, the privilege of the far-famed writ of *habeas corpus* is not an infallible and self-executing protection against illegal imprisonment. It is a "mortal contrivance" which, as Mr. Justice Holmes (who, incidentally, spoke for the majority in the Ju Toy case) says of constitutional law in general "has to take some chances". Or, to put it more accurately, individuals on occasion have to "take some chances" with the writ. In the light of the ancient history and salutary office of this writ it is highly probable that Congress would give it appropriate place in our jurisprudence whether the constitution mentioned it or not. In fact it is doubtless true that a number of the protections of individual liberty which we fulsomely attribute to the magic words of our written bills of rights would be quite as adequately met if there were no bill of rights. The chief difference would be that the courts would lack reasonable excuse for sternly lecturing the legislature and would be wholly incompetent occasionally to throw statutory prescriptions overboard. On the whole the solemn sound of the judicial voice in argument and reproof is often genuinely serviceable.

Prohibition and Bill of Rights

Since the adoption of the eighteenth amendment and the enactment of the National Prohibition Act public interest in three items of the bill of rights has been quickened anew. These are the provisions relating to searches and seizures, jury trial, and double jeopardy.

"In the development of our liberty," Mr. Justice Brandeis wrote in 1921, "insistence upon procedural regularity has been a large factor. Respect for law will not be advanced by resort, in its enforcement, to means which shock the common man's sense of decency and fair play." This expression was used in a dissenting opinion in a case that had nothing to do with prohibition. A corporation had dismissed an employee for alleged fraudulent conduct. Thereafter representatives of the company entered his office, broke open his desk, blew off the doors of his safes, and abstracted his private papers. These they turned over to the Department of Justice for use in prosecuting the ex-employee for fraudulent use of the mails. Mr. Justice Brandeis called this theft, which clearly it was. In effect it was his view that the government should not be a receiver of stolen goods even for the good purpose of enforcing its criminal laws. The case attracted little attention. It was isolated, exceptional. Not many men, common or otherwise, were shocked by it, for probably very few men ever heard of it.

"The damnable character of the bootlegger's business should not close our eyes to the mischief which will surely follow any attempt to destroy it by unwarranted meddling." Thus Mr. Justice McReynolds, also dissenting, wrote in 1925. A motor car had been stopped and searched by prohibition officers without a warrant. Liquor had been found. Confiscation of the car and its liquid contents and prosecution of the bootleggers had followed. The only "cause" for the interception, search, and seizure flowed from the fact that some two and a half months previously the same prohibition officers had "negotiated" with the same bootleggers for the purchase of three cases of whiskey. The latter, probably scenting trouble, had not delivered. Was this an unreasonable search and seizure? The court held that it was not.

The case attracted wide attention. Many a common man's sense of decency and fair play was shocked. There were terrifying visions of wholesale and indiscriminate prying into motor cars halted upon the road by ever-present government agents. The thunder of James Otis in 1761 against the iniquity of the odious writs of assistance by which goods smuggled into the colonies were sought to be uncovered was almost heard again. In point of fact nearly all of this denunciation was born of distorted views of the meaning and consequence of the decision.

The difference in the area and the intensity of the "shock" produced by these two decisions had little to do with the point of law that was involved. Men do not become excited about the effect of "procedural regularity" upon the "development of liberty" except as the regularity affects a liberty that is widely cherished and threatened. John Adams to the contrary notwithstanding, the thrilling effect of Otis's notable speech was due less to the quality of its oratory than to the fact that it voiced men's minds. Incidentally this "prelude of the Revolutionary drama" was not born in abstraction. It was pronounced in protest against a procedure which, however detestable, was entirely legal at the time; and the principal objection to it was that it made it more difficult for the colonists to violate a perfectly valid law which, not without justification, they heartily hated. Is there here something of analogy and possibly of lesson?

The use of the mails for purposes of fraud is universally condemned. It may be regrettable, but it does not greatly stir men's spirits to learn that the government employed evidence supplied by a thief to secure a conviction of fraud. The use of intoxicating liquors for beverage purposes is not universally condemned. And it stirs the spirits of many men to learn that even a perfectly legal procedure, let alone one of questionable legality, is being used to secure convictions. Emotions are not the stuff of which nice legal reasoning is made. This is at least one of the reasons why the search and seizure provisions of the National Prohibition Act have been subject to some popular misconstruction.

As a matter of fact our "castles" are rather securely protected by that Act. Home manufacture of intoxicants is indeed prohibited. But this is mere declamation; for no search warrant may issue to search a private dwelling unless the premises are being used for the unlawful *sale* of liquor. Moreover it is a criminal offense, punishable by heavy penalties, for any officer of the government to search a private dwelling house without a warrant.

Searches and Seizures

THE LIVING CONSTITUTION

By reason of these procedural restrictions "cellar and attic" manufacture for personal consumption is, so far as the statute is concerned, completely barricaded against invasion.

This is not true, however, of other buildings or property. Under the statute these may apparently be searched without a warrant provided the search is not made "maliciously or without probable cause". The Supreme Court has not yet passed upon the constitutionality of this provision as applied to buildings other than dwellings, probably for the reason that warrants are usually secured by the enforcement officers. But as to motor cars, boats, and other conveyances, the above mentioned decision settles the question of constitutionality, as well as the question as to what Congress meant by the somewhat ambiguously phrased statute. A search warrant is not necessary.

The argument runs that since goods in course of transportation can be readily put out of reach of a search warrant, a "reasonable" search within the meaning of the constitution may be made without such a warrant. As to the soundness of this distinction opinions differ. No doubt it has some basis in reality. There is, however, no occasion to put contraband goods out of reach of a search unless there is reason to suspect that a search is contemplated. If the danger is believed to be imminent, it is almost as easy to whisk the skulking goods out of a stationary hiding-place as it is to move a vehicle of transportation upon which they have been loaded prior to the rise of any suspicion that a search is about to be made. However that may be, such is the distinction that is made; such is the established rule of the law.

It cannot be too greatly emphasized that the popular resentment in some quarters of searches and seizures in liquor cases is not justified by the interpretation that has been put by Congress and the Supreme Court upon the constitutional guaranty of freedom from unreasonable searches and seizures. Had the Court held that a motor car might, upon "probable cause" though without a warrant, be stopped and searched for counterfeiting tools or even for narcotic drugs, there would have been no great hue and cry. The resentment grows out of the nature of the subject of prohibition in relation to public opinion and the number of people who are directly or indirectly affected. The prohibition amendment and law attempt to settle by stern legislative fiat an issue of enormous social importance about which opinions differ widely, sharply, even bitterly. Considering the number and the quality of prohibition agents and the extensive scale on which the law is violated, it is highly probable that there are instances—perhaps many instances—of unreasonable searches and seizures which are not pressed before the courts for rectification. The repercussion of Supreme Court decisions is not always complete. (Minimum wage laws are still being enforced in some of the states, despite the solemn judgment of their unconstitutionality.) Moreover, even if the right to be free from "unreasonable" search were in every instance meticulously observed there would nevertheless be outcry. Laymen, especially incensed laymen, do not readily distinguish between the "unreasonable" policy of a law and its "unreasonable" procedure. There is no more telling way to attack a hated policy than to allege that the procedure for its enforcement violates a sacred and fundamental liberty. It is frequently and heatedly asserted that the eighteenth amendment has put the fourth amendment in limbo. The assertion is untrue.

Much has been said in praise and something in blame of the institution of trial by jury. Concededly it is not flawless in operation. But who can

BILLS OF RIGHTS

offer a superior substitute? "The more the operation of the institution has fallen under my observation the more reason I have discovered for holding it in high esteem." It is the weight of a great name rather than the length and profundity of the author's observation that gives interest to this expression. For Hamilton was only thirty when in 1788 he expressed this "mature" reflection in one of that remarkable series of newspaper articles which were later published as *The Federalist*. Of greater importance is the opinion of a modern student of the system, Chief Justice von Moschzisker, who wrote in 1922: "I have taken part, in one capacity or another, in the trial or review of thousands of cases, and this experience has given me faith in the jury system."

Jury Trial

For better, not for worse, the institution is tightly grafted into our jurisprudential system. In some of the states, especially as to civil cases, it has been modified in the interest of simplifying and expediting litigation. It has been circumvented in certain state laws by a euphemism called a "civil forfeiture", which is in all truth nothing more nor less than what our forefathers called a fine. The action is "civil"—in both senses of the term. There is no criminal odium and no red tape of criminal procedure. Jury trial is often avoided; but on the whole the culprit is better off. Usually he cannot be jailed, although involuntarily he parts with his money to the government. Call it what you choose. The designation does not in any wise affect the fact.

In the federal courts, however, trial by jury has been preserved in all its pristine common law virtue. Twelve "peers" true and tried must unanimously agree, no matter how difficult it may be on occasion to win over an objector who through conscience or perversity is not unwilling to spend an additional night or two away from home.

Now jury trial is the pet abomination of the heedless prohibitionist. In the regions where enforcement of the law is most difficult it means delay in drawing juries. This increases court congestion. It means difficulty in securing convictions. This increases the number of violations. Summary process would be far more effective. But the constitutional guaranty of jury trial stands adamant.

The statistics of criminal conviction under the National Prohibition Act are impressive. There were nearly forty thousand in 1925. But it is significant that an overwhelming majority of these—ninety percent at least—were secured upon pleas

BILLS OF RIGHTS

of guilty. Jury trial is evaded—to the advantage of both the government and the accused. To the advantage of the government, because it would be impossible to try by jury all who are caught in the toils of the law. The courts would be caught in toils even more grievous. To the advantage of the accused, because it avoids delay. Where the practice is well-established of punishing by fine only, it is easier and quicker to pay, cry quits, and be on the job again, than it is to await the slow process of a jury verdict. This is often true even when the evidence in the hands of the government is not unanswerable. In such instances forcing the plea of guilty with the club of the prisoner's constitutional right of jury trial may seem like ironical justice. But there is comfort in the practical certainty that actual innocence has seldom if ever been "blackmailed" in this fashion.

Even in the absence of known penalty practices pleas of guilty are not infrequently made only upon a "gentlemen's" understanding in respect to the penalty. The "right to dicker" becomes of more importance than the right to be tried by jury. This secondary right, however, derives directly from the primary right and from the government's desire in the circumstances to lessen the court con-

THE LIVING CONSTITUTION

gestion that jury trials entail. The accused can scarcely complain of the net result. His right remains inviolable if he elects to avail himself of it. Certain it is that pleas of guilty rarely if ever culminate in jail sentences.

Padlock Practise

One other procedural practise under the Prohibition Act deserves mention. This is the "padlock" practise. It is accomplished by a civil not a criminal action. The government goes into a court of equity, where juries are unknown, and secures from the judge an injunction. This injunction runs for a fixed period—say six months or a year. It is directed to the owner or lessor of premises where, in restaurant, hotel dining room, or so-called night club, the government has proof that liquor has been sold. It enjoins not the mere sale of liquor but the operation of the restaurant, dining room, or club for any purpose. The offending door is thereupon battened and padlocked.

This procedure is interesting to examine. It is new to American civil practise. Contrast its appearances with its realities. The government possesses evidence of a criminal offense. It proceeds by civil action. This is swift. It is indeed incredibly swift, for the government always proceeds by agreement with the offender. (He cannot be called

BILLS OF RIGHTS

the "accused", for the action is "civil".) Having agreed, he does not attempt to refute the government's evidence. The case is over in a trice.

Why does the offender agree? Because, failing to do so, he is threatened with criminal prosecution and particularly with a probable sentence of imprisonment. If it were only the fear of a fine, he would not agree; for a fine would be far less serious either in amount or annoyance than the consequences of the padlock. The government, in other words, swaps with the offender immunity from possible imprisonment for his non-resistance to—one might almost say his collusion in—injunction proceedings. What is the net result?

To the offender the decree of injunction is manifestly in the nature of a fine, often an extremely heavy fine. To the government it is not; for the government collects nothing. The economic waste is patent. The law calls the premises a nuisance. This is the theory upon which the injunction may issue. Clearly this is fiction. The sale of liquor may very properly be declared a nuisance. But the premises as such are no more a nuisance than other similar premises where liquor is not sold. By what possible reasoning, moreover, can it be adduced that the quality of nuisance in a

THE LIVING CONSTITUTION

thing is purged by the lapse of six months or a year? Can the law make time perform magic?

To those who cherish affection for frankness and fairness in criminal procedure, whatever may be their views on prohibition, there is something palpably offensive about this process. In the guise of civil action it is undeniably a criminal prosecution with certainty of conviction. As has been said, in a criminal action under the Prohibition Act the accused who is faced with the prospect of fine only, passes up his right of trial by jury with a plea of guilty. He has no complaint. In this civil action the offender who is faced with the prospect of possible imprisonment passes up his right of trial by jury in a criminal action by agreeing to a fine that is often far larger than any that is contemplated by the law. Out of fear of the risk he barters away his constitutional right. Has he no ground for complaint? He has.

Double Jeopardy The prohibition amendment grants to Congress and the states concurrent powers of enforcement. Most of the states have enacted enforcement laws. Some of these outrun the national law in severity. Others parallel it. New York repealed her law on the subject. Maryland never enacted one. The Nevada law was on technical grounds held invalid.

BILLS OF RIGHTS

The fifth amendment of the national constitution declares that a person shall not "be subject for the same offense to be twice put in jeopardy of life or limb." Is this "great principle of action, sanctioned by humanity and justice," violated if a person is prosecuted under a state prohibition law and is also prosecuted under the national law for the same act? The Supreme Court has held that the principle is not violated by such double prosecution. This conclusion was doubtless inevitable. As far back as 1852 the Court said: "Every citizen of the United States is also a citizen of a state or territory. He may be said to owe allegiance to two sovereigns, and may be liable to punishment for an infraction of the laws of either. The same act may be an offense or transgression of the laws of both." In other words a single act may be two offenses. This construction of the word "offense" is open to some criticism; but it has been unvaryingly applied by the Court whenever the occasion has arisen, which has not been often. The decision as to prohibition statutes merely applied a long established rule of construction.

However consonant with the legal theory of federalism, this rule is repellent to many people's notion of common justice. Moreover, if double prosecutions and punishments are in order, should they not be regularly rather than very exceptionally undertaken? The fact is that for the vast majority of offenders the present cry of double jeopardy is a tocsin of phantom fear, though the situation may some day be otherwise. There are so many persons to be prosecuted once, by either the one or the other government, that neither government is likely to go in for prosecuting large numbers of persons who have already been prosecuted by the other government for the same act. The offender who is the exception has grievance on a double score. He is not only doubly prosecuted but he is also singled out of many thousands for this fate. His one complaint is against the harsh rule of the law for anybody. His other is against the discriminatory, the occasional, policy of its enforcement by prosecuting attorneys. Again, however, such is the law; and such also is the exceptional practise.

So much for the particulars in the bill of rights that have been jostled into new life by the prohibition amendment and law.

It has been pointed out that the guaranty of due process of law has been considered far more

BILLS OF RIGHTS

frequently with reference to state action than in respect of national action. This is because the police power is possessed by the states in such large measure and by the national government in relatively limited measure. As to the latter government it has been invoked chiefly, though not exclusively, in connection with Congressional enactments under the commerce clause. For example, in restricting interstate carriers to reasonable rates, Congress cannot authorize the fixing of rates which are said to be confiscatory. A reasonable return on the investment must be allowed. What is reasonable and especially how the amount of the investment is to be estimated are complicated questions. But the broad principle is clear: to deprive carriers of reasonable earning power is to deprive them of property without due process of law. This principle has been frequently applied.

Due Process of Law

In 1916 Congress enacted the famous Adamson Law by which the wages of employees represented by the four great railway Brotherhoods were, in effect though not in terms, increased during a period of months pending an investigation. The Supreme Court was asked to rule not only that this was not a regulation of commerce but also that, even if it were, it lacked due process.

This the majority declined to hold. But three justices dissented. It was their view that "Congress upon the face of the enactment expresses its inability to fix in advance of investigation a just and proper wage for the employees concerned". Meantime the cost of the experiment was to be borne by the carriers whether they could in fact afford to make the increase or not. Nor were they permitted to raise their rates to cover the increase.

These are examples of how the question of due process can be and is raised in respect of acts in regulation of commerce. On the other hand, the minimum wage law enacted for the District of Columbia was referable not to the commerce power but to the fact that the powers of Congress over the District are unenumerated. It was the due process guaranty that felled this law.

It is impossible here to illustrate the many kinds of state action that have been and are being questioned under the due process and equal protection guaranties. Some of them have already been referred to. As our economic society has become more and more complex, the states have laid restrictive hands upon an ever increasing number of human activities and relationships. They have sought, often tardily, to ameliorate certain eco-

BILLS OF RIGHTS

nomic conditions. They have endeavored in one or another way to protect the weak against the strong, to guard the consumer against the predatory monopolist, the fraudsman, the ravager of health, the debaucher of morals. They have dealt with the problems of race against race and of citizen against alien. They have attempted to prevent the waste or diversion of natural resources in private hands. They have imposed limitations upon the uses of private property to the end that the interests of the public might not be wholly ignored in the pursuit of private profits.

Much of this legislation, however well-intentioned, has been of crude quality. Too often it has been produced by inexpert legislatures composed of second-rate lawyers and of lay members who were wholly innocent both of the law and of the intricacy of the problems in hand. And almost invariably they have played the game of lawmaking, where heavy property interests were at stake, with a sometimes invisible but always powerful lobby of the interests on the sidelines.

Be that as it may, the Supreme Court is often asked to declare that legislation of the general varieties indicated operates to deprive persons, who are adversely affected, of their rights under the due process and equal protection guaranties. Rarely is it alleged that the state is depriving one of life without due process; but in many cases the Court is requested to void this or that law of a state on the ground that it invades the constitutionally protected domain of liberty and more especially of property and equal protection. As applied to laws enacted for the protection of labor "liberty of contract" has been a favorite and sometimes a telling invocation. This doctrine of liberty of contract the courts have derived from the due process clause.

These few paragraphs are utterly insufficient to characterize this nebulously comprehensive clause of the fourteenth amendment. Perhaps what has been said is almost meaningless to those who know little of the details of its unfolding at the hands of the courts. But the subject is large. It can be expounded only by citing numerous concrete illustrations. Generalities, whether from the pens of judges or other commentators, are little more than rhetoric. They do not illumine the meaning of due process and equal protection. It must suffice to say that this clause, as applied to the states, is the most important item in the bill of rights. Certainly it is the most fruitful of litigation.

BILLS OF RIGHTS

"It is the peculiar virtue of a written constitution," said Mr. Justice Brewer in 1908, "that it places in unchanging form limitations upon legislative action, and thus gives a permanence and stability to popular government which would otherwise be lacking." However unchanging the form, it is the peculiar virtue of our bills of rights that their substance has changed and is changing —never suddenly or violently, but ever by gradual interpretative process. It is not to be denied, as Lord Bryce once wrote, that these bills are "the legitimate child and representative of Magna Charta and the English Bill of Rights." But if the barons of Runnymede or the Whigs of 1689 could awake from their eternal sleep they would see in their progeny many more acquired than inherited characteristics.

Changing Bills of Rights

Chapter IV

The Presidential System

It has been said that "the one feature which distinguishes presidential government from the parliamentary or cabinet system is the almost complete isolation of the executive branch from the legislature, and its independence of the same body in respect to its tenure and powers." This embodies the usual unreality of most unadulterated legalisms. It would indeed be difficult to formulate a more inaccurate statement of the essential element in the distinction. Under the presidential system the executive branch is not in fact almost completely isolated from the legislative; and it is not independent in respect of its powers. Under the parliamentary system legislative and executive functions are not "inextricably commingled"; and in practise the cabinet is by no means always dependent upon the legislature in the matter of its tenure and powers.

"The executive power shall be vested in a President of the United States of America." With this

THE PRESIDENTIAL SYSTEM

declaration the second article of the constitution opens. It appears to settle with admirable brevity and finality the place of the President in the scheme of things political and legal. He is to be the Chief Executive; and from the beginning he has in popular parlance borne this title. To a very considerable extent, however, this is gentle fraud upon ourselves. The prime function of the President is not executive at all. It is legislative.

True enough the constitution vests "all legislative powers" in Congress. It purports to withdraw the President from his major executive role and to put him upon the legislative stage in only three minor and exceptional roles. He may call Congress in extraordinary session; he may deliver messages; he may veto proposals of law which, if Congress is still in session, may be passed over his veto by a two-thirds vote of each house. Popular demand for the appearance of the President in these lesser parts leaves him little time to star as Chief Executive. Politics has transformed his minor into his major role. The exceptions to his activities as Chief Executive are more important than the constitutional rule.

President as Chief Legislato

Moreover, this transformation, this inversion, of the office did not wait the slow progress of time.

The presidency was birth-marked for change in this respect as it came into being. No President who has, for whatever cause, attempted to self-abnegate himself as leader in the legislative program of Congress and to immolate himself upon the altar of executive duty has been aught but relatively ineffectual.

Nor is there cause for wonderment in this. It is simply a fact that the policies of government that enlist popular interest are mainly legislative policies. Executive policies are of small moment. Even the effect of administrative scandals is fleeting. Our presidential campaigns, to the extent that they are conducted upon any clear-cut issues of policy, are fought out normally upon the record of legislative achievements of the administration in power and proposals for constructive legislation ahead. We elect the President as a leader of legislation. We hold him accountable for what he succeeds in getting Congress to do and in preventing Congress from doing. Once in office, except for considerations of the patronage, which is politics rather than executive business, the time and thought of the President and his Cabinet are devoted far more largely to legislative than to executive matters. This is true even when Congress is not in session.

In the light of his apparently insignificant legal powers over action by Congress, this may seem unfair. In a way it is. But this must be said: The President does not lack means of making his own position on policies of legislation perfectly clear to the public. It lies largely with him to determine where the onus for unpopular action or inaction shall rest—whether upon him alone, or upon Congress alone, or jointly upon both. Fair or unfair, the fact is fact. And history does not record many instances of available candidates who shun or shy this high office because of the injustice of its exactions—or for any other reason.

That foreign affairs have played a conspicuous part in recent presidential elections does not alter the situation. To be sure the conduct of foreign relations has usually been regarded as an executive function. It has, however, never been a matter exclusively within the sphere of the executive, especially in the United States. And nearly everywhere, Mussolini's Italy to the contrary notwithstanding, it is becoming more and more a subject of legislative interest and discussion, if not of positive legislative domination.

The President, then, is a Chief Legislator rather than a Chief Executive. Moreover, this results not

THE LIVING CONSTITUTION

only from the practise of politics but also from law. The constitution vests executive power in the President. But Congress vests executive power nearly everywhere except in the President. Whenever an office is created its powers and duties are determined by statute. The incumbents of executive offices look to the law, not to the President, for the source and scope of their authorities. Such statutes, it is true, make liberal use of the phrase "subject to the direction and control of the President"; but the day by day activities of the several branches of the administration are in fact carried on quite independently of the President.

President as Chief Executive

The kernel of the President's power to direct and control is his power to remove. In legal theory therefore—indeed in legal fact—he may control the discretion of most administrative officers. In practise the opportunity to control this discretion does not often arise. There is no legal right of appeal to the President by parties in interest. Appeal, if any, lies only through the channel of publicity. Questions of executive policy may be brought to the President by the heads of departments; but needless to say questions that reach the President by this avenue are those which have actual or potential political significance. Questions of this character are also forced upon his reluctant attention by the ubiquitous gentlemen of the press, whose kindliness and friendliness vary from time to time. These are the ways, and they are practically the only ways, in which the President's power to control the discretion of executive officers is invoked. The use of the power is, therefore, exceptional even though on occasion dramatic. To conceive the President as the general manager of a vast administrative organization with his hand of control resting day by day upon all of its ramifying parts is to imagine a vain thing. The interregnum which was all but complete during President Wilson's long illness offers proof enough if proof were needed. The executive wheels of government did not stop. Indeed, except for the extraordinary international situation and for the fact that the law requires the presidential signature upon many documents, little administrative difficulty or embarrassment was encountered.

Such is the nature of the American presidential system in action. To say that it embodies an "almost complete isolation of the executive branch from the legislature" is to look no further than the letter of the constitution. It is to ignore the fact that the dead bones of the fundamental law

THE LIVING CONSTITUTION

are quickened into being by the flesh and blood of politics. Or, to change the metaphor, one might almost say that it gives a geographical interpretation to the constitution; for it sees nothing beyond the fact that the President and Congress sit at opposite ends of Pennsylvania Avenue.

We say that our constitution embodies the principle of the separation of powers. In modified form it does. But if it is true, as Mr. Justice Holmes has said, that "the fourteenth amendment does not enact Mr. Herbert Spencer's *Social Statics*", it is equally and much more importantly true that the constitution as a whole does not enact M. Montesquieu's *L'Esprit des Lois*.

Parliamentary or cabinet government is not a thing of type and uniformity. There are striking differences between the system as it operates in Great Britain and the British self-governing dominions and the system as it works in the countries of continental Europe. Some of these differences are attributable to constitutional arrangements and some to party divisions. Details cannot be given here. For the most part attention will be directed to the British system, the parent of them all; although it should doubtless be said in passing that cabinet government in one form or another pre-

THE PRESIDENTIAL SYSTEM

vails in most of the countries of Europe. In the new governments that arose out of the wreck of the War presidential government found no favor.

Writing in 1866 Mr. Bagehot defined the British Cabinet as "a committee of the legislative body selected to be the executive body." As descriptive of the "living reality" of the constitution no better illustration could be adduced of the "literary theory", "irrelevant ideas", and "inapt words", which Mr. Bagehot himself so trenchantly traduced. It is true that the members of the ministry (more numerous than the Cabinet proper) are legally the heads of the several executive departments. But the fact is that the Cabinet is a committee of the legislative body selected primarily to lead the legislative body. The members of the Cabinet devote themselves in very slight measure to executive management. The permanent undersecretaries are to all intents and purposes the department heads. It is highly probable that the administrative questions that are brought to the attention of members of the Cabinet and especially to the Cabinet as a whole are few and far between. It is very nearly certain that they are confined to such as have or may have political consequences. "The government of Great Britain," say Sidney

Cabinet as Leader of Legislation

[121]

and Beatrice Webb, referring to the executive branch of the government, "is in fact carried on, not by the Cabinet, nor even by the individual ministers, but by the civil service, the parliamentary chief of each department seldom intervening, except when the point at issue is likely to become acutely political." If this be true, as it indubitably is, it is manifestly misinforming to speak of the Cabinet as a committee selected to be the executive body. This is legal theory, not reality.

The ultimate aim, then, of both presidential and parliamentary systems is to set up legislative leadership. They differ (1) in the method of choice, (2) in the degree of effectiveness of the leadership, (3) in the relation between the leaders and the led, and (4) in the times and manner in which the electors are "consulted".

Choice of Presidential Leader

The American method amounts in substance to the popular nation-wide election of the President to be the legislative leader. Except where an incumbent, seeking reëlection, has made himself the leader of his party by reason of his office, candidates who are put forward for the presidency are seldom if ever *the* recognized leaders of their respective parties. Certainly Parker was not in 1904, nor Taft in 1908, nor Wilson in 1912, nor Hughes

THE PRESIDENTIAL SYSTEM

in 1916, nor Harding nor Cox in 1920, nor Davis in 1924. The nomination of Bryan in 1900 and again in 1908 was the nearest approach we have had in recent years to the choice of a candidate who, not having been President, was looked upon as leader of his party. Even as to Bryan there was sizeable disaffection within the party.

The reason for this is plain. There commonly is no single person who is admittedly the party leader. And the reasons for this are equally plain. The President himself, whether or not he actually leads with distinction, monopolizes the place of leadership in the party in power. Whether sphinx or oracle, feeble or strong, politically sage or politically inept, he occupies the post of vantage. No other can rival him; for he speaks from an eminence which no other can reach; and he wields numerous weapons which no other can grasp. He is all-absorbing, even in the transparent disguise of "Whitehouse Spokesman".

The opposition has practically no opportunity to develop a truly national leader except in Congress. And the disorganized and decentralized methods by which congressional business is carried on are not well adapted to the purpose. Moreover, the major parties are at best little more than

THE LIVING CONSTITUTION

loose federations of state or sectional parties. The Republicanism of Mr. Elihu Root is joined in unholy party wedlock to that of La Follette and Brookhart. The evangelical, white-supremacy Democracy of the South locks intimate political arms with the Irish-Catholic Democracy of Tammany Hall. This may be as it should be, or as it must be. It is certainly better than a regime of numerous closely knit small parties, with the European bloc system as the inevitable result, though truth to tell it is not wholly dissimilar. At any rate, these party facts are reflected in the halls of Congress. They do not make readily for unitary leadership. Hence the parties in nominating for the presidency turn to "available" men—to those who have attracted something of the nation's attention (and nothing of the whole nation's opprobrium) by accomplishments within the limited bailiwicks of the states. Or else they turn to an important "strategic" state where, the parties being evenly divided, they hope to transform defeat into victory by appeal to local pride and sentiment.

Choice of Prime Minister The British Cabinet is a committee of the dominant house of the legislature, the Commons, headed by the Prime Minister. At the time of a parliamentary election in England it is usually

THE PRESIDENTIAL SYSTEM

well known who is the leader of each of the two or three major parties. At least the question of leadership lies among not more than two or three persons. In voting for members of the House of Commons the electors know approximately, and often certainly, who will be Prime Minister in the event their party secures a majority of the parliamentary seats. Their ballots are cast almost as definitely for a specific candidate for Premier as American ballots are cast for a specific candidate for the presidency. The salient difference is that the party leadership of the British candidates is an established fact prior to the election, while party leadership attaches to the American candidate only if he is successful at the polls. The Premier is legislative leader because he is party chieftain. The President is party chieftain because the office makes him legislative leader.

Why this difference between British and American politics in the matter of party leadership? A number of reasons may be assigned. Mention has been made of the fact that the presidential office engrosses the leadership of the party in power. There is small opportunity for the emergence of an understudy. This is not nearly so true of parliamentary government, which is essentially far

British and American Contrasts

[125]

more collective in character. Centralization in the legislative process under cabinet government conduces to the development of leadership both in the party in control and in the opposition. Presidential government makes for decentralization in the legislative process. But these are probably the only reasons that may be ascribed to differences that inhere in the two systems. There are others of far greater importance.

Great Britain is small, compact. The United States is vast, diffuse, diversified. British parties are in consequence far more tightly held together. No change to the parliamentary system in America would alter our social and economic sectionalization. Something may be ascribed also to our federalism. In Great Britain service in the national government and especially in Parliament offers the only opportunity for ascent into leadership. The substantial powers of our states make possible the rise of local stars whose light is heard of, even though not seen, in remote parts of the nation.

But by far the most important reason for the difference lies in the fact that British Prime Ministers have almost invariably been chosen from what Sir Sidney Low calls an "actually large, but relatively small, governing class, consisting of the

THE PRESIDENTIAL SYSTEM

few thousand representatives of the nobility, landowners, capitalists, and leading professional men, who make up London society". He goes on to say: "Of the prime ministers of the nineteenth century the greater number were peers, or closely connected by birth with the peerage, like Grenville, Portland, Liverpool, Grey, Melbourne, John Russell, Aberdeen, Palmerston, Derby, and Salisbury; two, Peel and Gladstone, belonged to wealthy mercantile families; but Addington was a son of a physician, Canning's father was an obscure barrister and his mother an actress, and the elder Disraeli was a Jewish literary man of foreign descent with a name which most Englishmen were unable to pronounce correctly."

Undoubtedly change is taking place. No peer has been prime minister since Lord Salisbury. Nor, in view of the emasculation of the powers of the Lords in 1911, is one likely to become the leader of a party. Nor is any party leader likely to accept a proffered peerage if he has aspiration for the premiership. Generally speaking, however, Prime Ministers are still chosen from the upper stratum of English social life. To this class belonged Balfour, Campbell-Bannerman, Asquith, Bonar Law, and Baldwin. Lloyd George and Ramsay Mac-

THE LIVING CONSTITUTION

Donald are of course the striking exceptions of recent years. Both are of humble origin and traditionally quite outside the English governing class.

In the United States we have nothing whatever that corresponds remotely to a governing class. Potential leadership in politics is widely scattered. It lies in the lap of the gods. The suggestion was made at the time of the establishment of the Rhodes scholarships that one object aimed at was to bring the future political leaders of England and America together at Oxford during their formative years. The suggestion was grotesque. There is no way in the United States of handpicking the leaders of a coming generation from our numerous colleges. Cleveland, McKinley, and Harding never graduated from college.

In weighing the merits of the methods of constituting legislative leadership under parliamentary and presidential governments, the differences between British and American politics just mentioned are of consummate importance. If we put aside for the moment consideration of a definite term of office, the popular election of the Prime Minister upon a nation-wide vote would not greatly alter the British system. The complete transfer of legislative leadership from the President to a committee of the House of Representatives captained by a Premier (one or the other house would of necessity be largely subordinated) might or might not fundamentally alter our method of choosing a leader. If political parties did not nominate candidates for the premiership in advance of congressional elections, the new system would be not only revolutionary but also of highly doubtful efficacy. The voters would ordinarily choose members of the House without any knowledge as to who would occupy the post of primacy. Elections would lack adequate national focus. Party platforms, even though greatly improved, would not fill the void. Whether our candidates for the presidency are or are not in fact party leaders, they are at least put frankly before the people as candidates for such leadership. Their personalities give nation-wide cohesiveness, interest, and scope to the contest. The voter, however limited in choices, is not balloting in utter darkness.

It is possible, on the other hand, that the cabinet system among us might result in developing conspicuous party leadership. But the odds are against this. The more probable outcome would be that political parties would do to the system just what they did to the electoral college system. Facing chaos and loss of strength by dispersion, and realizing the psychological indispensability of a central figure, they would by some means or other nominate candidates for the premiership in advance of elections. Such a candidate would be, except when seeking reinvestment with office, not an actual but a promised leader. Our method of choosing our legislative leader would not be greatly altered. But of course this is speculation. If it did not befall, as it might not, more would be the pity —and the disaster.

Under the multiple party system of continental countries the selection of the legislative leader is manifestly different from either the British or the American plan. The leaders of the several parties are indeed generally known at the time of elections. But which of them will ultimately grasp the uneasy scepter is not known. That depends upon relative party strengths in the legislature and upon cloak-room bargains and compromises.

Source of President's Power

In the matter of effectiveness of leadership there is no question that the British cabinet system outstrips the presidential, just as there is no question that the American system outruns the usual cabinet system of the continent. The President's

THE PRESIDENTIAL SYSTEM

power is after all chiefly the power of publicity. Directly and indirectly he can argue and plead with members of the legislature in private. He can use several varieties of threat and he can veto. But his slightest utterance is headline news. That is his principal whip. And his success or his failure depends almost wholly upon the dexterity and wisdom with which he wields it. Rightly or wrongly the whole country looks to him, praises or blames him, for what Congress does or does not do, except of course when one or both houses chance to be in control of the opposing party. The political fortunes of congressmen and senators of his own party rise or fall with the market quotation of his popularity and strength, except, again, where sectionalism within the party or the party's overwhelming predominance in state or district emancipates a member from this entanglement. The President has also available the flail of the patronage which he may grant to or withhold from members; but the actual utility of this as an instrument of compulsion is probably exaggerated. Certainly it is less efficacious than formerly.

Such is the source of the President's power to lead. It derives less from law than from inescapable fact. National leadership, if not indispen-

THE LIVING CONSTITUTION

sable, is undeniably desirable. It is logical that the President, the only officer elected on a nation-wide vote, should gather in the reins—or to use more modern vernacular, take the wheel. But the situation is manifestly precarious. His legal powers are not commensurate with his political responsibilities. He needs a rare combination of personal qualities; and the effectiveness of the leadership demanded of him hangs upon numerous subtle, elusive, and changeful factors.

Source of Cabinet's Power

Quite otherwise is the situation of the British Cabinet. It is not only legislative leader; it is for all practical purposes the legislature itself. It is very nearly true to say that the laws are enacted not by the Commons at all; they are enacted by the Cabinet subject to the criticism and in extremely rare instances to the veto of the House of Commons. So keen-eyed an observer as Mr. Bagehot could not fail to note this. Despite his definition of the Cabinet as an "executive body" he said in another connection: "In England a strong cabinet can obtain the concurrence of the legislature in all acts which facilitate its administration; it is itself, so to say, the legislature." The sixty years that have unrolled since this was written have witnessed a slow and varying but almost steady in-

THE PRESIDENTIAL SYSTEM

crease of this predominance of the Cabinet over the Commons. And every competent commentator has recorded the fact. "Its own servants have become, for some purposes, its master," wrote Sir Sidney Low in 1904. "The ministry is the real law-making organ.... It can count on the support of its parliamentary majority for any legislative project, as long as the majority holds together."

The summit of Cabinet ascendancy was naturally reached during and immediately following the World War. In 1921 a Liberal critic, Mr. A. G. Gardiner, wrote: "It is a fact of universal admission that the prestige of the British Parliament has not been at so low an ebb in living memory as it is today.... The House of Commons has lost its authority over the public mind and its influence upon events." Naturally also, however, the Cabinet lost some of its primacy during the premiership of Mr. Ramsay MacDonald, for the Labor Party had no majority in the House; it was in fact second in strength. But with the tremendous Conservative victory in 1924, although the party polled an actual minority popular vote, the Ministry of Mr. Baldwin swung once more into the saddle. Cabinet supremacy, Cabinet mastery, was immediately restored.

Parliamentary government as practised in England is, then, more effective in the matter of leadership than is presidential government under the American scheme. But it is open to question whether it is not too effective. Intelligent Englishmen often deplore the low estate of the Commons as a body. "Government by discussion"—to use Mr. Bagehot's phrase—is conspicuous by the infrequency of its appearance. On the other hand intelligent Americans (usually, however, according as they are for or against the President's policies) deplore now the ease, now the difficulty, which Congress experiences in shaking itself free of the President's grip. And they especially lament the manner in which Congress falters and flounders when, having declared its independence, it appears to be utterly incapable of substituting effectual leadership of its own. Political systems rarely offer a choice between the wholly good and the wholly bad.

Presidential Responsi-[bility
In striking the contrast between presidential and parliamentary government great emphasis is commonly laid upon the matter of responsibility. The President is said to be completely irresponsible, the Cabinet completely responsible, to the legislature. This is exaggeration. True we move by

THE PRESIDENTIAL SYSTEM

the calendar in four year cycles. Once in office, a President can be got rid of only by impeachment. Legally he can during his set term be as irresponsible to Congress as he chooses to be. But practically he can ordinarily do nothing of the kind. His own and his party's assets are a common investment in which the members of his party in the legislature have a large stake. He cannot safely make use of this fund in disregard of the common interest. Nor can he safely commit it to the exclusive custody of the party membership in Congress. A President may assert partial irresponsibility in either of two ways. He may abdicate his leadership in large part, letting Congress go its own blundering way. This was the policy of Mr. Taft, of Mr. Harding, of Mr. Coolidge. Mr. Taft met his Waterloo in 1912, although under unusual circumstances. It is impossible to say what the fate of Mr. Harding would have been had he lived; certainly the large vote for his successor is no indication. Political prophecies are hazardous, but the alibi of nearly one and a half terms in office will probably be used to shut Mr. Coolidge gracefully out of the nomination in 1928.

A President may also assert partial irresponsibility by attempting to take over very nearly the whole of the job of Congress. This was the policy of Mr. Roosevelt and of Mr. Wilson. Had the former not previously renounced renomination in 1908, it is by no means foregone that he would have fought his Congress with such vigorous vetoes toward the end of his term. Had the latter not been physically ill and had he stood for reelection in 1920, his overwhelming defeat is as certain as any conjecture can be. At best, however, none of these Presidents pursued a course of total absence of responsibility to Congress. A President acting in complete disregard of his party in Congress would be an intolerable liability. Of course, if he lacks a majority in either house both responsibility and leadership tend toward eclipse.

Cabinet Responsibility

Legally the British Cabinet may in effect be dismissed by an irate or disgruntled House of Commons in the twinkling of an eye. Actually the Damoclean sword above its head is suspended not upon a hair but upon a chain forged of the stout steel links of machine politics. Possessing a workable majority in the House, the Cabinet is normally in little danger of the sword's descending. And for good and sufficient reasons. In theory the defeat of a Ministry by adverse vote in the Commons may result in their resignation and the

THE PRESIDENTIAL SYSTEM

formation of a new Cabinet drawn from the opposing benches. In the practise of many years such a defeat has always resulted in dissolution and a new election. To vote down the Ministry is to vote one's self out of a seat and one's party out of power. It is to play with uncertainty, to stake the future on a problematical throw of the political dice. Small wonder that the Commons is docile under domination. Cabinet responsibility is a threadbare legal conceit. At most it bespeaks a relationship that blossoms into reality only in high emergency, only in last resort. A Prime Minister sprung from a substantial majority sits his seat as firmly and as irresponsibly as any President. Moreover, while he sits, he leads, he governs, with a hand of authority that the President can seldom match. He does not await the strike of an election clock that is periodically timed. He awaits other toward or untoward events less regular, more sporadic in origin. Look at recent history.

Mr. Asquith (now Lord Oxford and Asquith) voluntarily ordered the two elections of 1910, one in January, the other in December. They were contests between the Conservatives and the Liberals over the question of subordinating the House of Lords; but they did not emanate from the

Recent British Elections

Prime Minister's responsibility to the Commons. Indeed they were forced by the Lords rather than the Commons. With the change in the midstream of the War (1916) from Mr. Asquith to Mr. Lloyd George the Commons had little if anything to do. The "khaki" election of December, 1918, was Lloyd George's personal mandate for an almost certain personal triumph. The inevitable political reaction following the War (revealed in adverse by-elections from 1919 to 1922) he ignored with quite as snug security as any President, possessed of an indefeasible term, might ignore unmistakable straws in the wind or even the midterm overthrow of his majority in Congress. But Lloyd George went on ruling. The hand had been long in writing—much too long as events proved —before he ordered the election of November, 1922. But it was not his responsibility to the Commons or any important repudiating vote of that body that precipitated the election. It resulted from his false assumption that the country was still back of him and that he could by an election victory silence his critics, chiefly out of Parliament. The Conservatives won and Mr. Bonar Law, his erstwhile coadjutor in the small War Cabinet, succeeded him as Premier.

THE PRESIDENTIAL SYSTEM

In a few months Bonar Law resigned on account of illness, and Mr. Stanley Baldwin took his place without election. In the autumn of 1923 he decided to have an election on the issue of a protective tariff. His decision was as voluntary as it was politically unsagacious. At this election no party secured a majority of the seats. The Conservatives were strongest, the Laborites next. Mr. MacDonald as leader of the latter took the helm in January, 1924. His position was naturally unique among recent Premiers. He had no majority. He ruled by the sufferance of his political opponents, or more accurately by the fact of their incompatibility. They had little to lose, perchance something to gain, by voting him down. They did so in October of the same year.

With a good deal of justification he might have picked up the precedent where Gladstone had left it in 1885; he might have resigned without asking for dissolution. But he elected to appeal to the voters. As a result of three-cornered contests in numerous constituencies, the Conservatives with an actual minority of the voters secured a huge majority of the seats. Thus was Mr. Baldwin reinvested with the robes of office.

In the light of this recent history it is untrue

to say that the British Cabinet ordinarily operates under hair-trigger responsibility to the Commons. Such a situation will result only if the abnormal tri-party division of 1924 becomes normal. Something corresponding to the instability of the Cabinet in France and certain other continental countries will then ensue. Curiously enough responsibility in such circumstances flows not from the existence of a master but from lack of one. "No man can serve two masters." But where multiple parties prevail, cabinets are nevertheless constrained to this impossible task.

Our Clocklike Elections

In the United States the voter is automatically consulted once in four years on the choice of a legislative leader. Twenty months after the leader's term begins on the fourth of March, it is predestined that his record be submitted in a fashion for the approval or disapproval of the electors when they elect congressmen and a third of the senators. The arrangement is clocklike. No heatwave of politics can alter its mechanism. No amount of political contentment can postpone its inevitability. Nor can discontent advance its hour.

At these elections, and particularly at presidential elections, a magnificent symposium of issues is offered for the voters' consideration. The past

THE PRESIDENTIAL SYSTEM

is exalted and damned; the future is safely and sanely pledged and hedged. Party platforms and campaign eloquence cannot be adequately characterized here. But this may be said: The major parties almost invariably straddle major issues. They do not divide on prohibition, woman suffrage, the League of Nations. Thus indeed they survive—by keeping somewhat but never very far apart on matters that enlist and divide the voters. For a vote is a vote, no matter whose it is or why. And victory is the ultimate goal, the end in itself, no matter how little actual solidarity of interest and conviction on the part of the electors it may represent. All is medley, with the leaders of the orchestra ringing the changes upon innumerable minor themes. Only rarely is a large question of policy —the gold standard, or tariff—allowed to become *the* issue of the campaign between the principal parties.

Now English parties also straddle important issues. Mr. Asquith was able to decline to make woman suffrage a proposal of his Liberal Government even after a majority of the Commons and of his Cabinet were openly committed to the cause. But when the voters are consulted in Great Britain they are usually, though not invariably, asked to pass judgment upon a single question of importance. Other issues may play some part in the campaign; but it commonly centers around one primary issue. It is more like a referendum upon a proposed law.

It may be plausibly argued that, in view of the number and variety of problems with which modern governments are dealing, it is right and proper that a hotchpotch of issues should be served up to the voter. But everybody knows that he cannot and does not digest the dish. He merely becomes either mentally obfuscated or bored. There is indeed distinct advantage in the one-issue-at-a-time scheme. It is perhaps the largest merit of the British system. Even so, the absence of something comparable in the United States is due much more largely to the deliberate strategy of parties than it is to anything that inheres in the presidential system. There are nearly always one or two issues of importance that could be made the pivot of the election if the parties were not in a kind of involuntary and fear-born collusion to prevent this.

Presidential System Assessed

There is much to be said, then, in vindication of the presidential system—at least as applied to the United States. It enables the parties to put forward candidates for legislative leadership where no actual leader of the party exists. Unless candidates for the premiership were similarly nominated in advance, our national politics under a parliamentary regime would no doubt be far more disorganized, disjointed, disintegrated, than they are at present. For national elections would be conducted with little or no centrality of interest and of purpose. Indeed the formation of sectional and other small parties would be a highly possible outcome. Only the innocent, the wicked, or the stupid would be willing to exchange presidential government for a galloping procession of impotent coalition cabinets after the pattern of the unstable European bloc system.

Something can be said, too, for a type of legislative leadership that is not superlatively effective. By and large stage-coach government is better suited to the spirit and the health of democracy than steam-roller government. It groans and creaks and lumbers, and it gets on but slowly. But it gives opportunity for discussion and for some popular enlightenment. A mediocrity as prime minister would probably light as pale and ineffectual a fire as have our mediocrities in the presidency. But a superman is safer for the country as president than he would as premier, at least under the two-party system. Whether he wills to or no, he is compelled to give and take pause.

Nor is there any great hurt in the two-year, four-year periodicity of our election system with its interim security of tenure. It may be argued that as Prime Minister Mr. Roosevelt would not have been turned out of office in 1908; but had he not "abjured the crown", he could probably also have retained the presidency. It may be urged that as Premier Mr. Taft would have been retired from office after the election of 1910 instead that of 1912; but it may be answered that as Premier Mr. Taft in all likelihood would have been able to forestall the fatal election far beyond November, 1910. The difference would have been that he would have continued in actual power, not being blocked and thwarted by a Congress of the opposing party. It is safe to hazard that Mr. Wilson as Prime Minister would have been restored to private life before the fourth of March, 1921. Probably he himself would have voluntarily advanced the date of the "solemn referendum" on the Treaty of Versailles. Otherwise he would have been forced to this step by an adverse vote.

This is not to imply that presidential government is a faultless political system. Far from it.

THE PRESIDENTIAL SYSTEM

But it is to say that all things considered it is doubtless better adapted to our needs than a parliamentary system would be. The fact that it is a system without honor save in its own country is neither here nor there. It is quite possible that some other countries might try it with profit.

The parliamentary system as exemplified in British practise is not without honor in the United States. There are some who apotheosize it. But realizing the obstacles in the way of accomplishing so drastic a change in the constitutional system, they urge a compromise. Let the members of the President's Cabinet have seats in the halls of Congress. Let them have power to introduce and defend administration bills. Let them meet Congress face to face. Let them have a forum in which to "speak their pieces". Let the whisper of "ear-kissing arguments" between administrators and legislators cease. Let "secret" relations between the President and Congress be routed into visibility. Let us have open legislation openly arrived at. Thus runs the plea for change.

Proposed Reform

In all truth and with due respect, much of this argument is sheer nonsense. Nobody has, or need have, any doubt about what bills are introduced or sponsored by the administration, except when the administration is seeking cover. The administration may come into the open and secure the fullest conceivable publicity for its proposals whenever it elects to do so. The forum of Congress is nowhere nearly so important as the forum of the press. And the President or any Cabinet officer has the press at his complete disposal whenever he has anything in defense or in mitigation to say—indeed all too frequently when he has little or nothing to say. The administration does not lack means of defending administration bills when it wills to defend them. It can complain not at all of being deprived of a market stall in which to exhibit its legislative wares.

Nor is it to be believed that this plan would assist appreciably in forcing a reluctant President into more visible leadership. Interpellations are an important feature of the British parliamentary system; but the Cabinet can and does hold interpellations in close rein because it largely manages the business of the House. If the members of the President's Cabinet had to reply on the floor to every attack that is now made upon the administration by congressman or senator, no time whatever would be left for the business of legislation. The practise of attacking and interpellating would

THE PRESIDENTIAL SYSTEM

have to be put in tight leash. And the members of the President's official family would, like the Ministers of the Crown, cultivate on a grand scale the fine art of polite evasion. Even at present the opposition, in matters of first-rate importance, can always drive the administration into speech or silence; and sometimes the latter is more revealing than the former. It is difficult to see how more could be accomplished by putting the combatants face to face in the arena. Moreover, it is childish to fancy that this would operate to abolish "private" negotiations around the President's breakfast table or behind closed office doors.

No doubt the plan would exert some influence upon the President's choice of Cabinet members. If it did not, one can but wonder how it would work with such men upon the floor as Albert Burleson or Josephus Daniels or Mitchell Palmer or Bainbridge Colby or Harry Daugherty or Curtis Wilbur or even Charles Evans Hughes. Nor is this to mention the manifest difficulty of seating the members of the Cabinet coincidentally in each of two jealously coördinate houses.

The late Henry Jones Ford, writing in 1918, said: "The specific demand for improvement in legislative procedure need, therefore, go no further than this: that the administration shall propose and explain all its measures—the bills and the budget—openly in Congress and fix the time when they shall be considered and put to vote. That is all, no more and no less." This sounds very simple. It is in fact far-reaching. One of the largest powers in the hands of the British Cabinet is its power to control and allocate the time of the Commons. Procedurally speaking, this is the very breath of its dominion. To vest in the President the power to fix the time for the consideration of and vote upon his measures could not end short of his assuming complete control over the entire legislative program of Congress. If important legislative initiative were presumptively left in Congress, it would of necessity be thrust aside. For the President's program would enjoy precedence and would lie in his own discretion. The only humanly possible result would be that the President would take the time of the houses into his own keeping. He would leave them such morsels as he chose. He would become exclusively responsible for the initiation and direction of all important legislation. The system would out-cabinet any cabinet system yet known, for there would be no emergency exit from a possible deadly deadlock. During four se-

THE PRESIDENTIAL SYSTEM

cure years Congress would do the President's bidding or nothing. Imagine the situation from June, 1919, to March, 1921, if Mr. Wilson had been able to control the time of the Senate! What would the "little Americans" have done? There might have been heads upon the green instead of only wigs.

Chapter V

Checks and Balances

CONSIDERING the forthright meaning of words the phrase "checks and balances" as applied to some of the devices of our government is not altogether happy. "Check" is indeed apposite. It denotes the restraint of one organ or unit of government upon another. But "balance" is defined as "an equivalent or equalizing weight; that which is put into one scale to offset the weight in the other". It implies equilibrium, statics, the delicate counterpoise of completely suspended action, entire absence of motion. Now some of our checks operate to produce balances of this kind; but they do not always have this effect. Sometimes one of the checking authorities outbalances the other and the result is action; not mere negation of action.

Thus when one of the houses of Congress refuses or fails to pass a bill which has been passed by the other, a balance is struck. This is the result also when the President vetoes a proposed law.

CHECKS AND BALANCES

But when Congress reenacts the law over the President's head, we have an example of a check that outbalances the veto check. When the courts declare an act of the legislature unconstitutional, there is a balance. But such decisions may be "checked" by the adoption of constitutional amendments. This is not infrequent occurrence under state constitutions, but it is exemplified under the national constitution only in the case of the successful income tax amendment and the unsuccessful child labor amendment. When the Senate refuses to confirm a presidential nomination for a vacant office, a balance results; but the President's power to make recess appointments is a check upon this check of the Senate. When the Senate declines to ratify a treaty negotiated and proposed by the executive, the ensuing balance can in no wise be overcome. The same is true when the legislature checks the executive by not voting needed supplies, by abolishing offices, or in extremely rare instances by the drastic process of convicting and removing upon impeachment.

Of course in a loose sense it may be said that in every one of these instances the will of one authority outbalances that of another. But let it be recalled that a balance is a weight that is put into the scale by one organ of government to bring another organ of government to a standstill. Its office is to produce inaction. Not all of our checks operate to this end. Which is only another way of saying that not all of our checks are absolute; a check sometimes checks a check.

Lord Bryce's View

It was Lord Bryce's view that checks and balances had no reciprocity of relation though both were designed "to safeguard the people against the consequences of their own ignorance or impetuosity." A check, he said, is a constitutional prohibition, "such as directing certain delays to be interposed or certain formalities to be observed before a decision becomes final, or by prescribing a certain majority as necessary for specially important decisions, or, in the case of a representative assembly, by excluding certain subjects from the range of its functions." A balance is secured by pitting one authority of government against another, and especially by requiring the concurrence of some other authority to give legal effect to the action of a legislative assembly. In other words, in his opinion a check is a check of words; a balance is a balance of authorities.

This seems rather questionable construction. As has been pointed out the restraining efficacy of

CHECKS AND BALANCES

mere words is not always overmastering when the power to interpret and apply them is not lodged in some external authority. Many of our state constitutions contain provisions "directing certain delays to be interposed and certain formalities to be observed" in the matter of making laws. Such prescriptions are in fact flagrantly flaunted by state legislatures, their journals of proceedings being piously forged to square with the prescriptions of the constitution. Since the courts cannot impeach the formal record of the journals this check of words becomes a travesty. It would seem, therefore, that constitutional limitations upon legislatures are usually translated into reality only when some other authority can reach out and enforce them. The check is the check of another authority. In this sense "checks" and "balances" are reciprocal words. The phrase means "checks and ensuing balances", even though, as indicated above, a balance does not always ensue. However, this may be, and probably is, superfinical quibbling.

In one of *The Federalist* papers Hamilton wrote: "The charge of a conspiracy against the liberties of the people, which has been indiscriminately brought against the advocates of the plan, has something in it too wanton and too malignant not

The Fathers' Intention

[153]

to excite the indignation of every man who feels in his own bosom a refutation of the calumny. The perpetual changes which have been rung upon the wealthy, the well-born, and the great, have been such as to inspire the disgust of all sensible men. And the unwarrantable concealments and misrepresentations which have been in various ways practised to keep the truth from the public eye have been of a nature to demand the reprobation of all honest men."

It must not be forgotten that this was written in a campaign document. Nor should it be overlooked that the debates and proceedings of the convention which drafted the constitution were during the campaign of 1787–88 and for many years thereafter jealously guarded as secret. It may be that the instrument was not a "conspiracy against the liberties of the people". That depends upon the definition of "liberties". But time has revealed—and many commentators have noted the fact—that the forethoughtful Fathers set about with great deliberation and intensity of purpose to bridle and curb the forces of democracy, to subject to the bit the dreaded tyranny of the majority. Certainly most of the checks that were introduced into the constitution were designed to this end.

CHECKS AND BALANCES

Thus the influence of democracy was to be filtered through the state legislatures by way of the electoral college to the presidency. It was to be sifted through the state legislatures to the Senate. It was to be further refined through these two distilled instrumentalities to executive officers generally and especially to the courts. And each of these organs, the President, the Senate, and the courts, was given checking powers of enormous importance. This was the design. What is the present-day result? Let the facts be faced.

The presidency, as we have seen, has been wrested by politics from indirection. The Chief Executive stands forth as legislative leader. When he exercises the veto power or otherwise promotes or forestalls legislation he may be either obstructing or reflecting the popular will. That depends upon whether he or Congress makes the better guess; and commonly both are sufficiently opportunistic when the public is in fact widely interested in a matter of legislation. It can scarcely be said, then, that the President's power in matters of legislation is either democratic or anti-democratic; and it may be neither the one nor the other.

Are Checks Undemo-[cratic?

Senators have been made subject to popular election. In spite of six year terms and partial renewal in the Senate in contrast with total biennial renewal in the House, it is open to question whether the lower house can be said to be any more eagerly responsive to public opinion than is the upper. Moreover, even if there were evidence on this point, due allowance would have to be made for the fact that the vote of one house is sometimes given with cunning calculation upon the probable attitude of the other.

When the Senate refuses to confirm a presidential nomination, it may or may not be reflecting public sentiment. In the head-on collision between President Cleveland and the Senate over appointments and removals in 1885–86, the Republican Senate, obviously sparring with a Democratic President for factional advantage, won little popular sympathy and support. The same was true of the defeat of Cleveland's excellent nominations in 1893 of Mr. Hornblower and Mr. Peckham for the Supreme Bench, which defeat was staged by Senator David B. Hill of the President's own party. The Senate's refusal to ratify President Roosevelt's nominations of one or two Negroes for appointments in Southern states was variously acclaimed and derided. The voting down in 1925 of President Coolidge's nomination of Charles

CHECKS AND BALANCES

Beecher Warren to be Attorney General—the only instance of the rejection of a Cabinet nomination since the heated days of Andrew Johnson—was probably approved on the questionable merits of the nomination but disapproved on the questionable policy of interference with the President's choice of his immediate official family.

Was the Senate's dissent to the Treaty of Versailles in or out of accord with the wishes of the people? That would be impossible to say. Had the treaty been accepted shortly after its submission, such acceptance would probably have met popular approval. But during the many months that preceded its final rejection it is no doubt true to say that it lost steadily in favor.

It is, however, especially the check of the courts that is looked upon as anti-democratic, and more particularly when this check operates to inhibit so-called social legislation. The theory of this check, as put forward at the christening of the constitution, is that it works to protect individual liberty, the liberties of minorities, against the cruel oppressions of majorities. "It is not otherwise to be supposed," wrote Hamilton, "that the constitution could intend to enable the representatives of the people to substitute their will [as expressed in

The Check of Courts

THE LIVING CONSTITUTION

statutes] to that of their constituents [as expressed in the constitution]. It is far more rational to suppose that the courts were designed to be an intermediate body between the people and the legislature, in order, among other things, to keep the latter within the limits assigned to their authority." If, in the judgment of the courts, there be conflict, "the constitution ought to be preferred to the statute, the intention of the people to the intention of their agents." In other words here was an ultra-democratic device. And this view of the function of the courts in voiding laws is often repeated down to the present day.

But manifestly there is supreme sophistry in this, however unintended. It would carry greater conviction if the constitution were so plain and explicit that the wayfaring man though a fool need not err therein. But the capital fact is that the most important parts of the constitution for this purpose are so inexplicit that the least nomadic of persons though a sage may very easily fall into error. The wisest and most learned of judges often spiritedly disagree. The courts are by no means simply an "intermediate body between the people and the legislature". They are certainly superior to the legislature. Hamilton said and meant that. But

CHECKS AND BALANCES

frequently also they are superior to the people, for the quite ungarnished reason that even when the people comprehend and approve the "intention of their agents", as set forth in this or that statute, they have not the smallest notion what their own "intention" was, as set forth in the constitution, until the courts have told them what they meant by the words they used. For that matter neither have the courts until they are called upon to give concrete pronouncement. Moreover, as we have seen, the controversy in many instances is not so much between the liberty of the minority and the power of the majority as between the liberties of one minority and the attempted assertion of the liberties of another.

Now the federal courts, by reason of the life tenure of judges, are fairly aloof from popular control; although by reason of the democratization of the appointing authorities—the President and the Senate—they are not nearly so aloof as Hamilton thought they would be. Moreover, it is absurd to think of judges as beings who keep themselves monastically distant from the moving current of political, social, and economic thought. They have nothing to gain and a good deal to lose in the repute which is dear to us all by being pur-

THE LIVING CONSTITUTION

blind reactionaries, impervious to the penetration of any thought more youthful than the stone age or even the age of Adam Smith. Nevertheless the courts do on occasion thwart the will of the people. The check of their veto is a restraint upon the forces of democracy.

The Supreme Court and Child Labor

Even as to this check, however, accuracy demands that one should speak with caution. It is quite possible that the judicial veto, like the executive veto, may at times more accurately mirror the public mind than the law which succumbs, though needless to say the courts do not declare laws void on the ground that they think the legislature has misjudged the popular will. Take the federal child labor laws. The first was enacted under the commerce clause, the second under the taxing power. Both were held invalid. A great hullabaloo was raised by the impatient reformers. Here was the reactionary Supreme Court again balking the will of the majority, again standing obstinately and obstructively in the path of progress. Whereupon Congress in June, 1924, proposed the child labor amendment. What was its fate? In 1925 it came before the legislatures of forty-two states. Twenty-two of them promptly voted it down. Seventeen took no action upon it.

CHECKS AND BALANCES

Only three ratified it. In Massachusetts where an advisory referendum was held the vote against ratification was overwhelming. Was this not fairly good evidence that public opinion, whether wisely or unwisely, was strongly opposed to a federal child labor law? Does it not show that, however unwittingly, the Supreme Court in this instance acted as a check upon the "anti-democracy" of Congress and the President?

Not many examples of this kind can be cited—perhaps no other among the relatively few laws of Congress that have been invalidated by the Supreme Court. As to a goodly number of these few there has in fact been no widespread public interest either pro or contra. The annulment of state statutes by the federal courts presents a somewhat different proposition from the viewpoint of democracy or undemocracy. From the New York steamboat monopoly law, declared void in 1824, to the Oregon law abolishing all private schools, judicially overthrown in 1925, there have been some notable instances in which the apostles of democracy have enthusiastically applauded the "vision" of the Supreme Court. In such instances the public opinion of the nation is, as it were, staked against that of a single state. The check of the Su-

THE LIVING CONSTITUTION

preme Court's veto happens to coincide with a national as opposed to a particularistic democracy.

From this brief glance at some of our more important checks and balances, is it not clear that there is something of fallacy in the almost universally accepted notion that these devices, whatever may have been their original purpose, always operate to protect the people against their own haste and folly? Often they do; but not infrequently they act to protect the people against the misguesses of their agents. Even the formidable and much vilified check of the courts occasionally officiates to this laudable end. Undeniably checks and balances slow up the process of government. Likewise they complicate it and help to screen responsibility. But it is false to assume that the people's one desire in politics is swiftness. And it is no less false to assume that the forces of democracy culminate in any one organ of government and especially in one or both branches of the legislature. Into the pitfalls of these assumptions stumble those who see nothing in our checks and balances but an unqualified repudiation of government by the people.

The merits and demerits of a legislature consisting of two chambers have been debated time

CHECKS AND BALANCES

out of mind. One trouble with much of this debate has been that it rests upon nothing more substantial than closet speculation. How could Mr. W. E. H. Lecky possibly prove that no form of government "is likely to be worse than the government of a single omnipotent democratic chamber"? If this be true Great Britain, with a greatly enfeebled upper house, must at the moment have a government which is very close to the worst possible type. James Kent cited no instances of "sad experience" to show that "passion, caprice, prejudice, personal influence, and party intrigue ... have been found by sad experience to exercise a potent and dangerous sway in single assemblies" as compared with double chambered legislatures. How could Lord Bryce demonstrate that the "innate tendency of an assembly to become hateful, tyrannical, and corrupt needs to be checked by the coexistence of another house of equal authority" —and (should he not have added?) of equally wicked innate tendencies. Are the evils of democracy to be cured by multiplying the agencies of evil and setting them against one another?

Check of Two Chamber

Another weakness in much of the discussion of the bicameralists is their failure to face frankly the question whether two principles of representation have need or right to seek and find institutional expression. In practically all of the countries of western civilization it is now conceded in practise that at least one house should spring from the ballots of a wide electorate. But if it be also conceded that birth and social station, or property, or eminence and experience, or local units of government in their corporate capacity, or functional or occupational groups, are entitled as such to coequal (or something not much more nor less than coequal) representation, the argument for two houses of legislation is fairly unanswerable. At least it is much simpler, and no doubt in other ways more desirable, to erect a special legislative body for representation of this kind. Fused into a conglomerate assembly both its virtues and its vices might be seen but darkly.

Now historically the bicameral system has had a variety of origins, which cannot be detailed here. But this may be said: in some instances, whatever the circumstances of origin, the system has rested upon a more or less definite theory of representation. It has been founded upon the belief that two different principles of representation should be realized in the political organization. On the other hand, in many instances precisely the reverse is

CHECKS AND BALANCES

true. The differences in representative principle if any—and not infrequently there are none of importance—have flowed wholly from the theory of bicameralism, from the belief that there ought to be two houses of legislation whether or not there are two different classes or things or whatnot to be represented. Manifestly in this latter case one very important prop for the system of double chambers is lacking. In modern times, in view of the wide acceptance of the broad general principle of democracy, nearly all of the arguments for two houses are based upon faith in the bicameral principle as such. Only those who, like M. Léon Duguit, urge the establishment of a second chamber for the representation of occupational or functional groups, proceed to the principle of bicameralism from a pre-proposed principle of representation.

Most of the new constitutions of Europe provide bicameral legislatures. Finland, Esthonia, and Jugoslavia are the only exceptions, while of the older governments, Norway, Bulgaria, and Greece are the sole exponents of the single chamber. Despite this fact, if recent constitutional developments be looked at in the large, it is probably accurate to say that the slow sweep of events is in

Decline of Second Chambers

the direction of single chambers. For in practically every instance the second chamber under the new governments is, in the matter of powers, not co-ordinate with but subordinate to the other and primary assembly. Cabinet government makes this almost inevitable. When a ministry is responsible to two coequal bodies and the two bodies disagree, one or the other becomes an intolerable nuisance; and responsibility becomes a serious joke—both for the ministers and for the country. A President in like circumstances can sit tight (and uncomfortable) and abide the fatalistic end of short terms of office. Somehow or other appropriation bills at least get through. But the whole genius of parliamentary government is opposed to deadlocks which might in some instances be of prolonged duration. Hence the tendency is to thrust the second chamber into the shadowy background of the crowded political stage.

The British Parliament Act of 1911 was admittedly a temporary measure. The ultimate constitution and status of the second chamber were to be determined later. There have been discussions and proposals; but the Lords still remain in the back seat into which they were ceremoniously ushered in 1911. Nor does it seem likely that they, or

CHECKS AND BALANCES

any other newly constituted chamber, are soon to be brought forward into any more prominent post of power than that which they now occupy. It would be a great mistake to imply that the Lords are wholly without influence in politics, or even that their influence is not often salutary. Concededly the upper house includes more men of parts than the lower. But to restore power to a once disempowered institution of government is a difficult psychological feat. Except in great emergencies democracies do not readily make restitution of their winnings. Or, as Lord Lytton lugubriously put it, "Democracy is like the grave—it never gives back what it receives."

Among parliamentary governments, then, bicameralism is of a certainty on the decline, though in numerous countries it will doubtless maintain its form and diminishing substance for many a year.

In the United States there is practically no agitation for converting Congress into a unicameral legislature. The difference in the principle of representation between the Senate and the House is a subject to which we will later advert. For the moment let us consider merely the operation of the check of one house upon the other. How effective is it?

Senate and House

THE LIVING CONSTITUTION

Probably not even experienced members of Congress could answer that question completely. Certainly no quantitative study of what each house does to the bills of the other would tell the whole story. For the houses do not work in sound-proof compartments. In all important legislation action is constantly taken by one house with knowledge or surmise or at least with hope concerning the action of the other, as well as the action of those ultimate and autocratic arbiters of differences, "conference committees". Even at close range the process is bewildering. It is impossible always to know which house is checking which. Of course some check results; but it is by no means certain that the house that is checked would not have checked itself had there been no other house.

Our legislative process is extremely loose. Initiation is unrestricted. Countless committees divide the labor of shaping bills. There is no complete centralization of authority and responsibility for a program. Party regularity in voting is far from regular. The Chief Legislator, the President, has legal powers that are not at all adequate to his political responsibilities. It is argued that on this account, if for no other reason, the check of one house upon the other is desirable, not to say in-

CHECKS AND BALANCES

dispensable. But this is to assume that the looseness of the process is inherent and that the bicameral system is its antidote. May it not possibly be that the looseness is the product of the system? Is it not possible, even probable, that a single house would organize and conduct its business in very different fashion? Assuredly the burden of the presidential role of leadership would be lightened for him and the role clarified for the public. As for the haste which the bicameral system is alleged to allay, what could possibly be more turbulently precipitate than the manner in which bills are speeded to the statute books in the dying days of an adjourning Congress?

But this is merely to fulminate against the impenetrable. The two houses of Congress are with us for a quite indefinite visit. If nothing else, the "vested interest" of the small states (no matter how radical otherwise) in their equality of representation in the Senate would stall any attempt at change. And no other vested interest is so firmly solidified into the constitution.

The movement for a single house of legislation has made some headway in a few of the states. Proposals to this end were voted down by considerable majorities in Oregon in 1912 and 1914, in

Oklahoma in 1914, in Arizona in 1916. Since these rebuffs discussion of the matter appears to have somewhat subsided.

Power of Veto Without the veto power it is safe to assert that the President would never have gathered legislative leadership into his hands. Or, to put it more accurately, legislative leadership would not have been thrust into his hands. It appears on its face to be a power only of negation, a power of destruction. But in the strange laboratory of our national politics it can be and has been, by competent modernists in the art of leadership, alchemically transmuted from brakes into steam. To be sure it cannot be used to start legislation on its way. But most of our important proposals of law do not flourish from seed to flower in a season. They are of relatively slow development. The time being ripe, there is no difficulty in getting any proposal for legislation started in Congress. To be sure also the veto power cannot be used to push legislative proposals to which Congress is indifferent or opposed. But such a state of affairs usually means public indifference or opposition as well.

It is when a measure is really under way, whether projected by forces in or out of Congress, that the President's veto power can be galvanized

CHECKS AND BALANCES

into constructive action. He can direct by threat, although of course the weight of his threat is measured by the degree to which he can convince the leaders in Congress that he reflects or can enlist public support. Inevitably also the imponderables of politics exert an influence upon the situation. At any rate, unless the President abdicates his leadership, the result is frequent negotiations between the White House and the Capitol during the progress of any important measure.

A bill, having passed both houses, is sent on to the President. Within ten days, if Congress be still in session, he may sign it; or he may allow it to become a law by simply letting the ten days lapse without affixing his signature; or he may return it to the house of its origin with the reason for his veto. In fixing this period of ten days the framers of the constitution doubtless intended merely to force the hand of the President within a reasonable time. But refusal either to sign or to veto has been used for other purposes. Presidents sometimes have sought by this means to escape positive commitment and thus to put the entire onus on Congress. In this attempt there is something of political casuistry. The measure has been put up to him. His action and his inaction have identical results;

THE LIVING CONSTITUTION

either one contributes to the making of the law. Perhaps there is no great objection to his selfrighteous indulgence in the inactive role; but it is difficult to see how he gains or should gain any considerable degree of merit thereby.

It is important to note that the President's power of veto is not in the practise of politics an absolute thing even when he knows that a two-thirds vote in each house cannot be marshaled to override it. Many a President has signed many a bill which he did not wholeheartedly approve. He has taken half a loaf or even an unpalatable loaf rather than no loaf. His negotiations may have convinced him that he has a choice only between something that partially meets his views and nothing. It is not always an easy choice. If he signs, he shares in and perhaps takes the major part of whatever opprobrium attaches. Even though he may not lack the opportunity to make his position unmistakably clear to the public, considerations of party fortune often prevent his doing so. If he vetoes, he unquestionably receives whatever blame there may be for inaction, even though Congress, having been warned in advance, is equally responsible for the failure of the legislation. Party platforms do not cry up the vetoes of

CHECKS AND BALANCES

the Presidents except where they have been registered against a Congress of the opposing party. Simple and straightforward as it seems, the veto is a device with many political ramifications.

If Congress adjourns within ten days after a bill has gone to the President the measure does not become a law without his signature. Since the date of adjournment is nearly always agreed upon well in advance of the date set, the President knows the bills to which this so-called "pocket veto" is applicable. It is absolute, not suspensory, for there is no opportunity for Congress to surmount it.

Under the usual practise the opportunity for the President to use the pocket veto with deliberateness and intelligence leaves something to be desired. Down to the administration of President Wilson it had been generally assumed that the constitution required the President to affix his signature to such bills as he approved before the actual adjournment of Congress. The last hours of the session are a hurlyburly of feverish energy. Numerous bills are being hurried relentlessly to engrossment. The President goes to his room at the Capitol to receive the legislative freshet. The clocks are turned back in unctuous defiance of the solar system. It is in such swift-moving circumstances that the President decides what bills he will put into his pocket, although of course with some of them he has had previous acquaintance.

In 1920 President Wilson extricated himself from this dilemma by inaugurating the practise of signing bills (within the ten day period) after the adjournment of Congress. Nothing could be more sensible; and certainly there is no clear constitutional inhibition, however contrary and long established the former practise had been.

It is obviously absurd to appraise the effect of the veto power of the President by counting vetoes. It is likewise absurd to say that because the veto is not often overridden it is in effect almost absolute. True it is, a two-thirds vote in each house is commonly not easy to obtain; but the apparent absoluteness of the President's interdiction as revealed by statistics is due to the fact that so many of his vetoes are of the pocket variety. Failure to override in such cases may be merely the result of the dilatory methods of Congress by which the passage of so many laws is clogged into the final days of the session.

The constitution declares that the President "shall nominate, and by and with the advice and consent of the Senate, shall appoint ambassadors,

CHECKS AND BALANCES

other public ministers and consuls, judges of the Supreme Court, and all other officers of the United States, whose appointments are not herein otherwise provided for, and which shall be established by law; but the Congress may by law vest the appointment of such inferior officers, as they think proper, in the President alone, in the courts of law, or in the heads of departments." *Check on Power to Appoint*

This familiar sentence is full of interest. For one thing, and quite unimportantly, it contains perhaps the only lapse from precision in the use of language that occurs in the finely written document, drafted under enormous difficulties in a brief period of four months. Not "officers" but "offices" are established by law. (The "committee on style" were master craftsmen at composition. If this be doubted one has only to compare our national constitution with any of our modern state constitutions or with any of the numerous recent European constitutions.)

The "advice and consent of the Senate" seems to imply an intimate communion between the President and the senatorial body as to whom he (it almost implies "we") shall have for officers. No President has ever lacked "advice" on appointments. But it has seldom if ever come from the

Senate as a body. Concerning appointments to nation-wide offices he takes his advice wherever he chooses—chiefly from those who are high in the ranks of his party or in his own personal esteem. On appointments to federal offices of state or local jurisdiction, he takes not only the advice but not infrequently also the ultimatum of the senator or senators of his party from the jurisdiction. For in this important matter the Senate is the closest of close corporations. The bitterest of political enemies within a party will usually stand as a unit on this prescriptive political prerogative, not knowing when they may need the like assistance of "dear enemies". The local prestige of having the power to dictate appointments is of greater importance than the urge to stand by the President for the national party weal. And naturally members of the opposing party will gladly support a badly treated fellow-member against his own leader. That is "human nature in politics".

This is called senatorial courtesy. The courtesy is not to the President. The check intended by the constitution is relocated. Individual senators do the nominating. The President can "check" only the outrageous. For the most part he is merely a transmitter to the Senate of a name that has been

CHECKS AND BALANCES

proposed by one of their number. Whereupon that august body ordinarily gives the "consent" authorized by the constitution, although the opposition, once certain that the right of the senator to nominate has been preserved intact, has then no hesitancy in bedeviling the progress of the confirmation if it so desires.

In 1906 before he became President Mr. Taft wrote: "A member of a community remote from the capital . . . wonders that a President, with high ideals and confessions of a desire to keep the government pure and have efficient public servants, can appoint to an important local office a man of mediocre talent and of no particular prominence or standing or character in the community. . . . [But] practically because of the knowledge of the senators of the locality, the appointing power is in effect in *their* hands subject only to a veto by the President."

As Chief Justice of the Supreme Court Mr. Taft wrote in 1926: "The rejection of a nominee of the President for a particular office does not greatly embarrass him in the conscientious discharge of his high duties in the selection of those who are to aid him, because the President usually has an ample field from which to select for officers, according to *his* preference, competent and capable men."

There is strange contradiction in these two utterances. This can be explained, if at all, only on the ground that in 1906 Mr. Taft was expressing the facts of practical politics, while in 1926 he was glossing the facts in order to sustain the legal theory of the President's complete responsibility for the faithful execution of the laws. Whatever the legal theory may be, there is no question that he wrote more realistically in 1906 than in 1926.

Congress, it will be noted, may provide for the appointment of "inferior officers" by the President alone, the heads of departments, or the courts of law. Relatively few appointments are vested in the President alone and practically none in the courts. A very large number are given over to the heads of departments; but most of these are now made subject to civil service requirements. In fact the civil service law and regulations constitute a highly important check which Congress and the President have imposed upon themselves.

The constitution does not define "inferior officers"; but the Supreme Court has said, curiously

CHECKS AND BALANCES

enough, that the term embraces all officers not specifically mentioned in the constitution. Ambassadors, other public ministers and consuls, and judges of the Supreme Court are mentioned. So are heads of departments, although senatorial ratification is not expressly required for these. Strange results flow from this quite unnecessary definition. For example the Under Secretary of State—the second ranking officer in the Department—is an inferior officer, but a petty American consul at Puerto Cabello, Venezuela, is not.

The constitution does not say, however, that the appointment of inferior officers may not be made subject to confirmation by the Senate. This is expressly left to the "proper thought" of Congress. And for patronage purposes, for the good of the party regardless of the health of the administration, Congress has thought proper to place the inexorable hand of the Senate upon many relatively inferior offices, especially those of local jurisdiction. It is in reference to these that the institution of senatorial courtesy operates.

It is of interest to note that the constitutional provision relating to appointments has influenced our institutional development in at least three significant ways. It has prevented Congress from providing popular election for important executive officers—members of the Cabinet, for instance. Thus has the national administration been spared this ill-laid element of decentralization which overtook most of the states. It has stopped Congress itself from making executive appointments. Directly or indirectly the President legally shares in every such appointment. It has frustrated the popular election of local national officers. The interposition of senators (and in default of these, of other local leaders of the President's party) has indeed introduced some element of decentralization. But this is as nothing compared with the dissipation of administrative responsibility that results in the states from the local election of officers empowered to execute many state laws.

History of Power to Remove

Attention has been called to the fact that the President's power of removal is the fulcrum of his legal power to direct and control the executive branch of the government. On the subject of removals, except by process of impeachment, the constitution is silent. Does the President derive this power by implication from the general constitutional grant of "executive power", or does it belong to him only by allowance of Congress and subject to such conditions and restrictions as Con-

CHECKS AND BALANCES

gress may by law impose? This question has been moot from the beginning of our history. Whatever its constitutional powers the practices of Congress have been various. For many years the President was, like interstate commerce, left "free and untrammeled" in this matter. In 1820 a four year term was prescribed for a considerable number of federal officers of local jurisdiction, such as district attorneys, collectors and surveyors of customs, registers and receivers of land offices. In the course of time limited terms were ordained for other similar officers and especially for postmasters who were in 1836 made subject to presidential nomination to the Senate.

Of course in one sense a limitation of term operates as a removal—a removal not made by the President. When a term expires the President may indeed renominate; but the Senate may refuse confirmation and thus in effect accomplish a removal. But manifestly the object of limiting terms of office was not to check the President's power of removal. The alleged justification was the democratic dogma of rotation in office. But the real object was to bring these offices actively into politics for the partisan use of both the President and the Senate by making periodical vacancies automatic.

Certainly that was the result, whatever may have been the purpose. And Presidents have not been heard to complain. They never thought of this as a restriction upon their powers. Quite the contrary. Moreover a fixation of term was never regarded as prohibiting a removal before the expiration of the term, although Presidents have no doubt frequently permitted the doom of an officer to be struck by the statute of term limitations rather than by a positive act of removal.

In 1867, during the administration of President Johnson, came the famous Tenure of Office Act. Conceived in hostility and born in hate, this law required senatorial confirmation of practically all presidential removals. The statute was modified under Grant and finally repealed under Cleveland, twenty years after its enactment. It was not declared to have been void until 1926—forty years after it had ceased to exist.

In the eighteen-seventies while this Act was still in force, Congress in excess of caution additionally provided that the President should take the "advice and consent of the Senate" upon the removal of first, second, and third class postmasters. These officers constituted then as now a group that far outnumber all other presidential appoint-

CHECKS AND BALANCES

ees combined. This law Congress never repealed. It may be that in the interim of nearly fifty years since its passage Presidents have occasionally removed postmasters without complying with this law. It is entirely possible that some Presidents have not even known of its existence. But during most of this period, as everybody knows, postmasterships have flourished as the richest and best crop of party spoils. The machinery used for harvesting was sometimes a request for resignation. Whether in ignorance of the law of 1876 or in deference to the "higher law" of party prerogative, such resignations commonly came promptly forth. More usually the President has pursued the practice of nominating a person to take the place of an incumbent. Confirmation by the Senate has operated not only to instal a new appointee but also to remove an incumbent. In fact, therefore, the Senate has by a single act consented both to a removal and to an appointment. Thus has the law of 1876 been generally complied with, though truth to tell the practice did not grow out of the law. As early as 1835 Webster declared on the floor of the Senate that this same practise in the matter of removals had been regularly followed since the beginning of the government.

In relatively recent years Congress has imposed a wholly different kind of restriction upon the President's power of removal. It has by law sought to give something of independence to certain high officers (however "inferior" in constitutional theory) by prescribing causes for which they may be removed during their fixed terms. Protection of this kind has been extended especially to the members of important commissions and boards, such as the Interstate Commerce Commission, Federal Trade Commission, Tariff Commission, Federal Reserve Board, Federal Farm Loan Board. Railroad Labor Board, United States Shipping Board, and the Board of General Appraisers. Some of these statutes have and some have not specifically declared that removal may be made only for the causes designated. But whether or not the statute attempts to fix the sole grounds upon which removals may be made, the prescription of limited terms and the laying down of causes for removal have apparently had a deterrent influence upon the President. At any rate in such circumstances the President has seldom if ever made removals.

Finally, in 1920–21, Congress prescribed a wholly unique method of removal. In the law creating the offices of Comptroller General and

CHECKS AND BALANCES

Assistant Comptroller General of the United States it was provided that these officers, appointed by the President and the Senate for terms of fifteen years, could be removed only by joint resolution of the House and the Senate for specified causes, or by impeachment. President Wilson vetoed this law on the ground that it unconstitutionally deprived the President of his power of removal. Shortly after the Harding administration began the law was reënacted and was approved by the President.

This, in brief résumé, unfolds the essential features of the history of congressional action in this matter. It tells nothing, however, of the oft-debated legal question concerning the source of the President's power to remove and the competence of Congress to restrain him in its exercise. Nor is it now important to review the few cases antedating 1926 in which the Supreme Court has expressed opinions on this or that aspect of the subject. Suffice it to say that down to October of that year the Court never passed upon the fundamental question: May Congress impose restrictions upon the President in this matter; if so, are there any limits to its power to restrict?

The 1926 Decision

This question came before the Court by reason

of an act of President Wilson in 1920. He summarily removed the postmaster of Portland, Oregon. He did not ask for his resignation. He did not follow the practice of nominating a successor whose confirmation by the Senate would operate to remove the Portland incumbent. He violated the law of 1876. Was this law valid?

By a vote of six to three the court held the law void. In the opinion and judgment of the majority the power of the President to remove any officer whom he nominates, and by and with the advice and consent of the Senate appoints, cannot be restricted by law. Otherwise, runs the main argument, he cannot adequately exercise the "executive power" which the constitution vests in him nor properly perform his constitutional duty to "take care that the laws be faithfully executed". Congress cannot require the consent of the Senate to the removal of such officers nor can any other statutory limitation be imposed. If the law specifies the causes for which removals may be made, the President may nevertheless remove without assigning any cause. This applies to all officers who are appointed by the President and the Senate with the exception of judges of the United States courts, who, by the constitution, "hold their offices during

CHECKS AND BALANCES

good behavior", and with the possible exception of judges in the territories and outlying possessions.

The ins and outs of this rather intricate constitutional question cannot be sufficiently discussed here. The difficulties that surround it are perhaps revealed by the fact that Chief Justice Taft, who spoke for the majority, employed twenty-two thousand words to explain why the President could not be restricted, while two of the dissenters, Mr. Justice McReynolds and Mr. Justice Brandeis, each required almost as many words to set forth the contrary view.

Speculation is rife as to what institutional effect this decision may lead to. The probability is that it will have no far-reaching effect. As to some presidential appointments the decision puts Congress, and especially the Senate, on the sharp horns of dire dilemma. To be sure Congress can by law surround those "inferior" officers who are not appointed by the President and the Senate with some protection against removal. But Congress can effect this only by providing that such officers shall be appointed by the President alone, by the heads of departments, and by the courts of law. Obviously appointment by the courts may be ignored. Apart from any other consideration to vest the

What will Congress Do?

power of appointment in the courts would be political self-denial beyond human capacity. To give the President exclusive power to appoint would destroy the Senate's jealously guarded power of scrutiny over presidential selections. The Senate knows all too well that this succulent power to consent to appointments yields far more in practical politics than the rather juiceless power to impose statutory restrictions on the President's authority to remove. Moreover the decision leaves the question open as to how far Congress may go in placing restrictions upon the removal of officers appointed by the President alone. The Senate therefore, however aggrieved it may feel at this decision, is not likely to relinquish a substantial political reality—its share in the appointing power—in order to assert an uncertain constitutional competence to limit the President's power of removing officers whom he is authorized to appoint without the Senate's consent.

Nor is it probable that Congress will make any wholesale transfer of the appointing power, as now prescribed by the statutes, from the President and the Senate to the heads of departments. This again would mean that senators would cease to scrutinize presidential nominations. They would

CHECKS AND BALANCES

no longer enjoy the experience of being "courteous" to one another in the high prerogative of backing up the demands of individual senators upon the patronage. Courtesy of this kind is far too precious a possession to be lightly tossed aside.

Moreover, Mr. Justice Brandeis to the contrary notwithstanding, there is at least one limitation which Congress may not impose upon the heads of departments in making removals. It may not require the consent of the Senate. As far back as 1866 the court felt "no doubt that when Congress, by law, vests the appointment of inferior officers in the heads of departments it may limit and restrict the power of removal as it deems best for the public interest." This view was not overruled by the decision of 1926; but it was narrowed. The majority declared quite emphatically that whatever other restrictions might be placed upon the removing power of department heads Congress could not by statute constitutionally require senatorial consent.

Congress, then, is not apt to make any radical change in the existing situation under which officers are appointed. But what of the President? Has this decision greatly enlarged his powers? In legal theory it unquestionably has done so. It gives

What will the President Do?

him full rein. He may retire every presidential appointee to private life at a stroke of the pen. He can be as capricious as he chooses to be. "Caprice" is more than once referred to in the dissenting opinions. But caprice seldom gets a President or anybody else anywhere. The history of the office shows that we may certainly count upon average intelligence and normal political acumen in the presidency. Prompted by this decision a bold President—a Jackson, a Lincoln, a Cleveland, a Roosevelt, a Wilson—may on occasion be bolder than he would otherwise be. But at best or at worst such instances will be only occasional.

The President now has it in his power to abandon the procedure of making removals by nominating successors whose confirmation by the Senate operates to remove incumbents. He may, if he elects to do so, now make the removal in advance of submitting a new nomination, even though the Senate be in session at the time. But manifestly the Senate in passing upon the new nomination when it is later presented has full opportunity not only to voice disapproval of the removal but also to harass the President by refusing confirmation. Meantime the office remains vacant. Moreover, in view of the established practice of allowing the

CHECKS AND BALANCES

individual senators of the President's party almost complete control over federal appointments in their respective states, it is difficult to see what the President will gain by making an opposed removal only to submit to dictation in respect to a successor in the office. As to such offices this decision may in rare instances invite the President to a show of pugnacity. But the removing and appointing powers are so closely tied together that by and large he will probably find no great comfort in making what is, after all, a fairly futile gesture of independence. Far from destroying senatorial courtesy the effect of this pronouncement, if the President acts upon it, will doubtless strengthen the practise, if that, indeed, be possible.

The provisions of law prescribing causes for which certain officers appointed with senatorial consent may be removed by the President have by this decision been swept off the statute books. The Chief Justice went out of his way to say: "There may be duties of a quasi-judicial character imposed on executive officers and members of executive tribunals whose decisions after hearing affect interests of individuals, the discharge of which the President cannot in a particular case properly influence or control. But even in such a case he may consider the decision after its rendition as a reason for removing the officer, on the ground that the discretion regularly entrusted to that officer by statute has not been on the whole intelligently or wisely exercised. Otherwise he does not discharge his own constitutional duty of seeing that the laws be faithfully executed."

Will this encourage the President to remove members of the Interstate Commerce Commission if he disapproves of a rate decision rendered by them? Or members of the Tariff Commission if his mind does not run along with theirs in respect of a finding and recommendation? Whatever the law, as thus expounded, the President will probably not often follow the indicated lead. He will not do so because of the nature of the duties that are imposed upon these important commissions and boards. The law of 1916 which created the Tariff Commission, provided for removal for specified causes. But even before the decision of 1926 the President, under the rule of a case decided in 1903, could nevertheless remove members of this Commission without naming any cause. Despite this fact President Coolidge, about to rename a member in 1926, asked the prospective appointee for his undated resignation. His request was very

CHECKS AND BALANCES

properly refused. But why was it made? Probably because the Republican President thought that the Democratic Commissioner (the law required a division of membership between the two parties) could thus be held to "sounder" views on the tariff; if this hope proved vain he could be ousted without the positive act of removal which might give rise to too great criticism. The President was apparently sanguine to believe that he could secure secrecy in the matter by springing an undated resignation which he had clubbed out of the officer in advance of his being nominated. In fact he secured neither the resignation nor the secrecy. But the episode illustrates the hesitancy which Presidents will undoubtedly always have in actually removing officers of this kind before the expiration of their terms. Viewed in the light of practical politics, this decision probably does not put the members of the several great national commissions in imminent jeopardy of presidential wrath. Nor does it place their offices in the category of legitimate political spoils following a presidential election.

As for the Comptroller General and his Assistant a President who summarily removes one of these officers must be not only brave and defiant but also ready for a fight to a finish. Congress does not lack retaliatory powers.

On the whole, therefore, it seems possible greatly to exaggerate the institutional consequences of this decision. Congress, if it be wise, will continue to impose restrictions on the President's power of removal whenever it deems restrictions expedient. These will not be legal compulsions but they may serve as moral guideposts —perhaps even as danger signals.

Check on Treaty Making

The constitution vests the President with "power, by and with the advice and consent of the Senate, to make treaties, provided two-thirds of the senators present concur". A treaty is a contract between two or more independent governments. But in effect treaties are also laws, often governing private rights and relations just as statutes may and do. Now it is conceivable that the legislature of one country might propose a treaty to the legislature of another country and that the proposal might pass back and forth between the two until its terms were finally agreed upon. This, however, would be an extraordinarily cumbersome and protracted procedure. Multitudinous minds do not readily meet at such long range. Contracts are more easily drafted by a few persons around a

CHECKS AND BALANCES

table. For this reason, as well as because the day by day conduct of foreign relations is almost of necessity committed to the executive, the negotiation of treaties is everywhere committed to the administrative branch of the government. The President initiates and carries on negotiations with foreign governments either through the Secretary of State or through a regular ambassador or minister or through one or more special commissioners.

Very exceptionally has a President taken the "advice" of the Senate as a body in advance of the negotiation of a treaty. But in such matters a wise President always keeps in close touch with the chairman and other members of the Senate Committee on Foreign Relations. The extent to which a few senators are thus drawn in on actual negotiations varies with time, circumstance, and President. This forward end of the job, however—the initiation, the bargaining, the drafting—is regarded as belonging peculiarly to the President and his agents. Then follows the check of the Senate. And a most formidable check indeed it has on occasion proved to be.

"A treaty entering the Senate is like a bull going into an arena; no one can say just how or when the final blow will fall—but one thing is certain—it

THE LIVING CONSTITUTION

will never leave the arena alive." This was the pessimistic view of John Hay, Secretary of State under McKinley and for a short time under Roosevelt. The statement is of course absurd, as Mr. Hay knew. The fact is that an almost negligible number of treaties submitted by the President have actually received a fatal stab by the Senate. A few of these, including the Treaty of Versailles, have been of very great importance. There has often been furious fight, but wounds and mutilation have been more frequent than fatalities; and the great majority have, with or without fight, come through entirely unscathed.

Amending Treaties — "Wounds and mutilation"—for the Senate asserts the right not merely to consent or refuse consent but also to "amend" proposed treaties. From one point of view this is a peculiarly insulting procedure—insulting both to the President and to the foreign state. And, perhaps naturally but none the less regrettably, it is being used with more contumely as the United States, sitting snug in the family of nations, becomes more and more puffed with prosperity, pride, and power. The situation is thus: The American and the foreign negotiators have sat. They have exchanged ideas. They have come to hand to hand agreement. They have

CHECKS AND BALANCES

drafted a document. This document the Senate receives. That body is securely isolated from the other party to the proposed agreement. It debates in spurious secrecy. It adds or subtracts or otherwise alters and sends the proposal back to the President saying in effect: "We give our constitutional consent with these changes which we have made." The President has the choice of dropping the disfigured proposal in disgust—which he occasionally has done—or of going back to the foreign negotiators with the word that "My overlord, the American Senate, demands these words or nothing." Which the foreign power may or may not be willing to accept.

The point is not that the Senate should abnegate its power or conceal its views. It is immensely important that a legislative body should pass upon treaties, which are nothing more nor less than laws. It is rather a question of international good manners. Why should not the Senate, without either giving or refusing consent, send the proposal back to the President with its suggestions, leaving the matter of drafting to the joint representatives of the countries whose joint law this is to be? Thereafter let the President, having renegotiated upon the Senate's suggestions, submit the proposal again for the Senate's consent in revised or unrevised form as the case might be.

It can be argued of course that the prevalent practise accelerates the business in hand. In a way it does, although, be it said, the Senate proceeds with such exasperating slowness as it chooses. The treaty with Cuba, ratified in 1925, which relinquished our claim to the Isle of Pines was before the Senate for twenty-one years. The Treaty of Versailles, rejected for the second time in March, 1920, was under senatorial consideration for eight months and was in fact politically before the country for many months thereafter. Compared with these Fabian examples, the delay of new negotiation and resubmission to the Senate would be quite inconsiderable. Under the existing system there is no question that foreign governments have from time to time reluctantly and not without some irritation accepted Senate amendments because of the need for the treaty and the lack of opportunity to argue out differences with this aloof and inaccessible body. It is a matter of unfair advantage in the method pursued. While the practise of submitting treaties to legislatures is developing in European countries, nowhere yet has the practise of legislative amendment been established.

CHECKS AND BALANCES

Perhaps by taking a lesson from the book of American senatorial practise foreign legislatures might also teach a lesson in international fair play.

As has been suggested there is ordinarily no smooth sailing to a two-thirds vote in the Senate. The requirement of the approval of treaties by a majority of both houses of Congress would, it would seem, better comport with the desideratum of democratic control of foreign affairs. This is especially true in view of the highly unequal constituencies from which senators spring, a subject to which we will return.

A good deal has already been said and something remains to be said later about our chief of checks, the courts. In our discussion of federalism we saw the nature of the check of the national government upon the states and of the states upon the national government—a check that arises from the constitutional division of powers between the two. These with the few that have been considered immediately above are the principal features of our check and balance system. Under the state constitutions a number of the same checks and balances are found with results in operation that roughly correspond to those which obtain in the national government. In addition a good many

THE LIVING CONSTITUTION

states have introduced the check of a general scheme of popular referendum upon laws.

Survival of Checks
In 1920, writing of checks and balances in general, Lord Bryce said: "Though experience shows that no nation has ever been cool enough and wise enough to dispense with some restraint on its impulses, the tide of fatalistic faith in the sovereignty of the people tends in nearly every country to sweep away such checks as exist, replacing them by no others; and the peoples who most need to be protected against themselves are the least disposed to provide such protection." There are in this the usual questionable assumptions: the note that in matters political the people would if they could act upon impulse alone, as swift and terrible as the sword of the Lord; and the further note that the check and balance system operates exclusively to protect the people against themselves, against the consequences of their own volatile folly. Nor is that all. Neither in the old nor the new governments of Europe can it be shown that the tide of fatalistic faith in popular government is tending to sweep away checks except the check of monarchy and hereditary aristocracy and to an extent the check of second chambers. As for the United States, despite relatively slight modifica-

CHECKS AND BALANCES

tions from time to time, and despite our recrudescent vocal explosions against the occasional concrete operation of this or that check, belief in popular sovereignty itself stands little if any higher in our accepted articles of political faith than loyal adherence to the check and balance system. This is by no means an outworn and abandoned tenet in our fundamentalist creed.

Chapter VI

The Representative System

MODERN governments must perforce legislate upon a wide and ever widening variety of subjects. The making of all laws by direct action of the people would be hopelessly impractical. Some sort of representative system is indispensable. Moreover, unless the representative assembly is to consist of a very few members, it is likewise indispensable that the people should, for the purpose of choosing representatives, be divided into groups of one kind or another.

Aims of Representation

Before discussing the American system of representation it may be well to ask a fundamental question or two. Is the representative supposed to reflect the views of the group that elects him, or, once elected, should he exercise independence of judgment? Is he supposed to represent his district or the nation as a whole? These closely related questions have been endlessly discussed.

"The people's power," wrote Lord Brougham, "being transferred to the representative body for a

THE REPRESENTATIVE SYSTEM

limited time, the people are bound not to exercise their influence so as to control the conduct of their representatives as a body on the several measures that come before them." "The representative should be a pillar of state," said Edmund Burke, "not a weathercock on the top of the edifice exalted for his levity and versatility and of no use but to indicate the shiftings of every fashionable gale." Addressing his constituency at Leeds in the campaign of 1832, Lord Macaulay declared that it would be absurd for the voter "to require positive pledges, and to exact daily and hourly obedience from his representative". Elect an expert statesman, he told them in effect, and leave him alone. In his treatise on Representative Government, John Stuart Mill devoted an entire chapter to the consideration of idealistic relations between constituencies and representatives. His views he summarized as follows:

"As the general result of what precedes, we may affirm that actual pledges should not be required, unless from unfavorable social circumstances or faulty institutions, the electors are so narrowed in their choice, as to be compelled to fix it on a person presumptively under the influence of partialities hostile to their interest: That they are entitled to a full knowledge of the political opinions and sentiments of the candidate; and not only entitled, but often bound, to reject one who differs from them on the few articles which are the foundation of their political belief: That in proportion to the opinion they entertain of the mental superiority of a candidate, they ought to put up with his expressing and acting on opinions different from theirs on any number of things not included in their fundamental articles of belief: That they ought to be unremitting in their search for a representative of such calibre as to be entrusted with full power of obeying the dictates of his own judgment: That they should consider it a duty which they owe to their fellow countrymen, to do their utmost toward placing men of this quality in the legislature: And that it is of much greater importance to themselves to be represented by such a man, than by one who professes agreement in a greater number of their opinions; for the benefits of his ability are certain, while the hypothesis of his being wrong and of their being right on the points of difference is a very doubtful one."

Views in the tenor of these just quoted are of interest in the realm of political idealism; but they are of little importance in practical politics. It

THE REPRESENTATIVE SYSTEM

boots nothing to admonish the voter about the kind of representative he ought to seek. There is no profit in warning him to respect the independence of his representative. And nothing is gained by lecturing the legislator concerning the weight he should give to the opinions and wishes of his constituents. Mill recognized this when he said: "Let the system of representation be what it may, it will be converted into one of delegation if the electors so choose." Well, the fact is that the electors do often so choose. Most representatives have their eye on reëlection possibilities. If an opinion is widely or strongly held among their constituents, they are likely to give ear to it and to act upon it. But this is not invariable. Senator James W. Wadsworth, for example, opposed the national woman's suffrage amendment after his state, New York, had by a large popular majority extended the suffrage to women. He was nevertheless reëlected, receiving the votes of many women.

Idealism and Practical Politics

The truth is that under every representative system the representative, though apt to respond to any generally prevailing opinion in his district, ordinarily enjoys considerable independence of his constituents. The problems he faces are numerous. On many of them his constituents have no very definite views. Campaigns are all too frequently conducted without clear-cut issues. Candidates can often avoid making embarrassing promises. It may be that better government would result if the people chose representatives solely with reference to their character and ability and not at all with reference to their views. It may be that, having robed these superiorities with the mantle of office, it would be well for people to give them implicit and uninterfering trust. But a complete experiment in that type of representation would probably have to wait the rise of a generation that had been taught to judge character and ability in men but had not been taught to read and write or to use the telephone and telegraph. It would seem that the degree to which representatives reflect the wills of their constituents should have steadily risen with the spread of popular education and the multiplication and improvement of media for organizing and expressing public opinion. But synchronously the problems of government vastly increased in number, in variety, in complexity. It has become more and more difficult for constituencies to develop coördinated public opinions upon numerous shifting political questions. The effectiveness of the force of more en-

THE REPRESENTATIVE SYSTEM

lightened public opinion is largely neutralized by constant additions to the heavy load it is, in theory, supposed to drive.

The point has often been made that members of the British House of Commons regard themselves as representatives of the nation rather than of particular constituencies, while the reverse is true of members of the American Congress. The usual reason assigned is that the American representative must commonly be a resident of the district from which he is chosen, while the English member need not be. Undeniably there is a difference in attitude of mind. But it is probably due in large part to causes other than this matter of residence. There is, for one thing, the already mentioned difference between the two countries in respect of size and compactness. The most widely separated of British constituencies are close neighbors as compared with Maine and California. More than this, Great Britain is far more homogeneous in point of economic problems. True there are industrial and commercial centers, mining, agricultural, and rural districts. But since the country does not sustain itself in raw products nor consume its own manufactured output, agricultural and industrial problems are more largely na-

Local vs. National Representa-[tion

tional than sectional in character. There is no great geographical contrast such, for example, as that between the cotton belt of the South, the coal and iron region of western Pennsylvania, and the great grain area of the Middle and North West. Social differences, too, while they are more firmly fixed than in the United States, are not to the same extent sectionalized. These facts make for a degree of national unity in party organizations that simply does not exist in the United States. It follows that the residence of a candidate in a particular section is of less importance than his acceptance by and his place in the party organization. It follows, further, that once elected, he looks upon himself as representative of the national party rather than the election district.

One other point: The British Parliament is not a great distributor of spoils to the local political units of the country. Members of the Commons have little or nothing to say concerning gifts of post-offices, customs offices, court buildings, army posts, navy yards, fish hatcheries, national parks, river and harbor improvements, reclamation projects, and the like. Whether the practise of the American Congress in such matters is a cause or an effect of the mental attitude of representatives and

THE REPRESENTATIVE SYSTEM

constituents toward one another it would be difficult to say. Perhaps it is both. But certainly the fact and the attitude are intimately related; and the fact does not obtain in Great Britain.

The British plan of not insisting upon residence in the district has one obvious advantage. An important party member, defeated in one district, can easily be returned from another. This has an important bearing upon continuity of party leadership; but it has little or nothing to do with the question here under consideration: What should the representative represent?

Whatever distinguished commentators have said to the contrary, the underlying assumption of representative government in the minds of most people—certainly in the United States—is that representatives are chosen to reflect the political beliefs and opinions of the groups that choose them. There is, however, often a yawning gap between the theory and the facts. This is due to varying causes which can by no means be adequately discussed here. It must suffice to indicate a few of them very briefly. *Theory and Facts*

Attention has already been called to several facts pertinent in this connection. It is well-nigh impossible that constituencies should have determinable views upon all of the numerous and complicated problems of modern government. Imminent issues are often deliberately dodged or sidestepped in party platforms and campaigns. In the resulting fog the voters do not know what mandate they are giving, nor the representative what mandate he is receiving. Moreover, even if clearly put forward, the issues are multifarious. A vote may be a blanket endorsement; but it is seldom if ever an intelligent expression of opinion upon and approval of the issues of the campaign one by one. Finally, elections often turn not upon what is proposed but upon the past record of the party in power. The voters do not cast ballots for A but against B. It matters little who A is or what he stands for or promises.

True enough, elections are not the only means by which the opinions of the constituency may be expressed. The newspapers of the district acclaim, condemn, threaten, advise. Chambers of commerce and citizens associations resolve and memorialize. The mailbags of legislators overflow. Telegraph and telephone lines hum. But these expressions may or may not mirror anything that may properly be called an opinion of the constituency. Sometimes they do; often they do not.

THE REPRESENTATIVE SYSTEM

These, then, are a few of the facts of politics that belie the generally accepted assumption that the representative is chosen to bear into the legislative chamber the political beliefs and opinions of his constituent group. A cardinal fact remains —the nature of the groups into which people are divided for purposes of representation.

The constitution requires that representatives be apportioned among the several states according to population. Congress requires that they be chosen in single member congressional districts. The state legislatures fix the district lines. The basis of the grouping is geographical. To what extent do these geographical districts actually result in grouping people appropriately for purposes of representation? That is a poser. For similar political views sometimes emerge from widely differing environments. There are radical millionaires; and there are highly conservative workingmen. But by and large political views are the reflexes of economic interest and of such factors as education and social background. A congressional district that covers only a farming community usually embraces a fairly homogeneous population. There is a minimum of division of labor, of diversity of economic interest, of social stratification, of differences in

Representation by Geographical Districts

education and wealth. The tendency is toward homogeneity of opinion. Certainly there is an element of common political interest growing out of common economic interest. Much the same thing may be said of a district that includes exclusively workingmen, especially if they are engaged in a single great industry. Even in these relatively homogeneous districts, however, such forces as race and religion often appear to have more cohering influence than stark economic interest.

But a very large number of congressional districts are not of this character. They frequently include both urban and rural communities or are carved quite arbitrarily out of the territory of large cities. Now in sizeable cities there is a maximum of division of labor, of diversity of economic interest, of social stratification. There are, it is true, rich and middle-class and poor residential sections; but these are rarely if ever consistently followed in dividing the population geographically into mathematically equal groups. Frequently they cannot be followed. Moreover, means of transportation and communication make possible opinion groups within the city that are almost wholly independent of neighborhoods. If neighborhood sentiment exists it usually flows from common ra-

THE REPRESENTATIVE SYSTEM

cial origin. It is often completely lacking. From the viewpoint of grouping people of common interests the districts are not infrequently superlatively artificial. If there are common interests and common views, the people of the district are at least wholly ignorant of the fact. They do not know one another's interests or views. A representative chosen from such a heterogeneous agglomeration of people cannot transmit the image of their group opinions. Such opinions do not exist. His chief index of their political thoughts is that, in electing him, a part of the district group—sometimes a majority, sometimes a mere plurality, which is a minority—have apparently put the stamp of their approval upon his all-comprehensive party label, which may or may not reveal much concerning their views.

Moreover, these bare majority or plurality elections are in themselves devastating proof of the illogical nature of these district groups as opinion groups. It is absurd to regard the victorious candidate as representative of a large minority or even a majority of his district who voted against him. These voters who cast ballots for unsuccessful candidates are without any direct representative. Their consolation, their recompense, if any, is that in other districts the tables were turned. Candidates of their party "carried" these districts in similar circumstances. Voters of the opposing party in such districts are, like themselves, in effect disfranchised. For among numerous districts, at least under the two-party system, the inequities more or less even up. Disfranchisement is not too strong a word to use in this connection; for the net result would be precisely the same if these unrepresented electors had no vote at all.

The geographical district plan of representation is ancient and simple. But manifestly a system that operates to deprive large numbers of voters of an effective ballot is inherently wrongful. Why, then, have we so long tolerated it? The answer is that the party division of voters at the polls infrequently represents a division of opinion that is fundamentally vital. There is little emotion in it and often even less of intense rational conviction. It is of no great moment which party wins. And in any case the totality of party representation is probably about what it would be if every vote counted toward the election of a representative. What is lost unfairly in one district is gained equally unfairly in another. Clearly, however, the system contributes something toward the emanci-

THE REPRESENTATIVE SYSTEM

pation of the representative from the obligation of reflecting the views, if any, of his district as a whole, whatever he may feel that he owes to the majority or minority who gave him support.

Such is the nature of our congressional district system of representation. And generally speaking state legislatures are chosen under similar systems.

It is usually assumed to be of importance that there should be approximate equality of population among the representative districts. In point of fact excessive nicety in this matter, based wholly on relative numbers and ratios, is little less than absurd. There is nothing whatever to the notion that every resident of every district should be hypothetically possessed of a fifty or a hundred or a two hundred thousandth part of his district representative. Only mathematical precisianists could entertain the idea that that is a matter of consequence. Politics and pure science are not only strange but also quite belligerent bedfellows.

Equality of Representation

Equality of district populations may or may not be of importance. That depends upon the character of the districts that are put in contrast. Here a representative is chosen by the almost unanimous consent of a fairly homogeneous district group. In a neighboring or far distant district of practically identical character, but of half or a quarter or of double or quadruple the population, another representative is similarly elected by overwhelming majority. What do the differences in numbers signify? Nothing whatever. But here is still another representative who has skimmed a scant plurality from a heterogeneously divided district. His actual supporters are a minority in his own district. Of what importance is it that the total population of this district equalizes with that of some district in which there is—to employ Mr. Giddings's phrase in a specialized connection—"consciousness of kind" and of interest? It is of no importance. Not total populations but total interest or opinion groups should, if anything, be equalized, if that were possible, which it is not.

Parity of populations among districts is usually of first-rate importance only when considerable disparity exists among aggregates of districts that differ quite obviously in economic and social circumstance. For example, great industrial centers may in proportion to their teeming populations be grossly under-represented. Cities may be discriminated against in favor of rural communities. A single city may be selected for specially invidious treatment. In such circumstances there is just

THE REPRESENTATIVE SYSTEM

ground for dissatisfaction. For despite the fact that there is diversity of political opinion in these areas, there is also a measure of uniformity of interest and of idea. If industrial centers are given their proportionate number of districts, the interests of labor will probably be more adequately represented than otherwise, no matter how arbitrarily and illogically the districts are formed. Toward many matters political there is certainly a general, if somewhat intangible, difference in mental attitude between urban and rural populations. Notwithstanding, therefore, the artificiality of many representative districts in cities, equality of district populations is of some importance when aggregates of this kind are considered.

Such disparities rarely if ever exist under our congressional district system. This is because reapportionment is periodically undertaken. The constitution requires that a census be taken every ten years and implies that Congress shall thereafter redistribute seats to the states. Districting is thus made to tread fairly closely upon the heels of shifts and growth of population. Chiefly because of unwillingness to increase the size of the House and of reluctance to reduce the representation of states which have lagged behind the national pace in increase of population, Congress does not always act with immediacy. Down to adjournment in 1926 there had been no reapportionment under the census of 1920. But compared with that of many countries our system is a model of swift response to fluctuations of population. In Great Britain, as has been said, there was no redistribution of seats in the Commons between 1885 and 1918—thirty-three years. In France the distribution of deputies remained static from 1889 to 1919—thirty years. The German revolution of 1918 obliterated a seating in the Reichstag which dated from 1870—a stretch of a near half-century. In all of these countries there had developed, meantime, enormous discrepancies in district populations, chiefly to the disadvantage of the laboring classes in large cities.

Most of our state constitutions likewise require a periodic reapportionment of seats in both chambers of the legislature. Single member districts are thus kept approximately equal in population. But in some of them, where township or counties are given equality of representation regardless of population, rural sections of the state are in contrast with urban vastly overrepresented. In a few New England states monstrous disproportions prevail. Moreover there is in some instances deliber-

THE REPRESENTATIVE SYSTEM

ate discrimination against large cities. These variations from equality are due in part no doubt to the prevalent notion that cities, and especially large cities, are both radical and vicious. The fact is that nearly every radical movement in American political history, from Jacksonian democracy to the North Dakota Non-Partisan League, has been of agrarian origin. And it has never been demonstrated outside of fundamentalist pulpits that rural peoples within the limits of their opportunities are far in advance of urban in point of virtue. Partisan politics aside, it is by no means certain that the political life of New York, Illinois, Maryland, and Rhode Island would not be benefited by giving New York City, Chicago, Baltimore, and Providence their legitimate representation in the state legislature even though it constituted a majority. Rural communities would assuredly fare no worse at the hands of city representatives than have the cities at the hands of rural legislators. They would probably fare better.

Two senators are chosen from each state of the Union, formerly by state legislatures, since 1913 by direct vote of the people. The states vary in population from 77,000 in Nevada to more than ten millions in New York. Nevada contains fewer

Representation in the Senate

people than Schenectady or Albany or Yonkers or Syracuse. Delaware holds fewer than Rochester. Nine states each—six of them west of the Mississippi—have smaller populations than that of Buffalo. Pennsylvania, Ohio, and Illinois are the only states that exceed New York City in population. The ten largest states comprise more than half the population of the entire forty-eight. The ten smallest states have less than four percent of the total—less indeed than any one of the ten largest. In the elections of 1922—an off-presidential year—less than 30,000 electors voted for senatorial candidates in Nevada, and less than 65,000 in Arizona, Wyoming, and Delaware respectively. But nearly two and a half million ballots were cast in New York and about one and a half million in Pennsylvania and in Ohio.

The shocking character of these mathematical inequalities might be illustrated with almost infinite variety. The point has already been made, however, that equality of district populations is of great importance only where aggregates of districts present striking social and economic contrasts. For example, Massachusetts, New York, and Pennsylvania are states with many similar characteristics. They are predominately industrial

THE REPRESENTATIVE SYSTEM

and commercial, and each has a metropolitan seaport that somewhat overshadows the rest of the state. In such circumstances it is perhaps of little importance that they are equally represented in the Senate although the population of Massachusetts is only about one-third that of New York and less than half that of Pennsylvania.

But the equality of states in the Senate does result in gross over-representation of an aggregate of agricultural states. With a few exceptions, such as New Hampshire, Rhode Island, and Delaware, it is the industrial states that are the populous states of the Union. The agricultural states are sparsely peopled. The census of 1920 shows that 51.4 per cent of the population of the country was urban. But there were only fifteen states—less than a third—in which more than half of the people lived in cities and villages. These fifteen contained slightly more than a half the population of the country. All of them except Colorado, Washington, and California were east of the Mississippi. Eight of them were on the Atlantic seaboard. The other thirty-three states, embracing less than half the total population, were predominantly rural. In nearly half of them rural inhabitants outnumbered urban by more than two to one.

The result is obvious. The agricultural peoples of the country have enormously more than their proper share of representation in the Senate. Rural thought, rural ideals, rural conscience, hover over a considerable majority of the senators, while the industrialization and commercialization of the country steadily progress, steadily draw into their vortex an ever larger percentage of the population. This explains why the stronghold of the so-called "farmers' bloc" is in the Senate rather than the House. A far larger proportion of senators than congressmen are chosen by votes from farms.

Some excellent senators have on occasion been returned from unpopulous agricultural states. That is beside the point. An excellent senator might on occasion be returned from any kind of pocket borough. But it is perhaps thought-provoking that our arch-isolationist, the trouble-making and diplomacy-bungling Chairman of the Senate Committee on Foreign Relations, Mr. Borah, sits his seat with the mandate of less than a hundred thousand voters residing in the seventh least populous state of the Union, Idaho, where nearly three-fourths of the people are farmers, fruit-growers, and cattle-raisers. Manifestly, however, an isolated example of this kind proves

THE REPRESENTATIVE SYSTEM

just nothing at all. Mr. Borah's predecessor, Mr. Henry Cabot Lodge, came from Massachusetts.

It was the thought in the beginning that the senators would represent the states as political units in what may be analogically called their corporate capacity. The two senators were not to vote as a unit, however, and they were not subject to instruction from and recall by the legislatures which chose them. Whatever there may have been in the original notion, it was swiftly and utterly annihilated by politics. The vote of one senator constantly nullifies the vote of his colleague from the state when the two are of opposing parties. This is, to put it mildly, a curiously futile method of representing a state in its corporate or any other capacity. Senators do not represent states. They represent their respective party groups within the States. Their popular election since 1913 only serves to emphasize this fact, which has prevailed almost from the outset of the government.

Writing in 1908, four years before his elevation to the presidency, Mr. Wilson said of the Senate: "What gives the Senate its real character and significance as an organ of constitutional government is the fact that it does not represent population, but regions of the country, the political units

Wilson on the Senate

[223]

in which it has, by our singular constitutional process, been cut up. The Senate, therefore, represents the variety of the nation as the House does not. It does not draw its membership chiefly from those parts of the country where the population is most dense, but it draws it in equal parts from every state and section. . . . Regions must be represented, irrespective of population, in a country physically as various as ours and therefore certain to exhibit a very great variety of social and economic and even political conditions. It is of the utmost importance that its parts as well as its people should be represented; and there can be no doubt in the mind of any one who really sees the Senate of the United States as it really is that it represents the country, as distinct from the accumulated populations of the country, much more fully and much more truly than the House of Representatives does. . . . The House tends more and more, with the concentration of population in certain regions, to represent particular interests and points of view, to be less catholic and more and more specialized in its view of national affairs. It represents chiefly the East and North. The Senate is its indispensable offset, and speaks always in its make-up of the size, the variety, the hetero-

THE REPRESENTATIVE SYSTEM

geneity, the range and breadth of the country, which no community or group of communities can adequately represent."

It is certain that Mr. Wilson would not have written in this strain after he had seen "the Senate of the United States as it really is" from the office of the presidency. Indeed, violently obstructed by the Senate, and thoroughly disillusioned by contact that was at once too close and too distant, he petulantly characterized the Senate toward the end of his office as "a little group of willful men, representing no opinion but their own."

However that may be, the view that he expressed in 1908 embodied a curious distortion of the facts. As has been pointed out, the Senate does not represent the "political units" into which the country has been cut up. It does not represent "the variety of the nation" to any greater extent than does the House, whose membership is also drawn from all parts of the country. It over-represents one variety and under-represents another. It does draw its membership "in equal parts from every state" but not in equal parts from every "section" if by section anything definitively logical is meant. It draws its membership most unequally from agricultural and industrial sections. Even if section is here employed in a loose geographical sense, as of North, East, South, Middle West, Far West, there is no equality of representation of such sections in the Senate. The House does not represent chiefly the East and North, unless such states as Ohio, Indiana, Michigan, Illinois, and Missouri are to be included in this designation. Even with these inclusions the "East and North" have only a very slight majority. The people of all the various parts of the country are undoubtedly entitled to some representation in any national legislative body. But if it is of the "utmost importance" that "regions" and "parts" should be equally represented irrespective of their populations, then without question the millions of acres of arid plain and timbered mountain in Idaho may lay just claim to two senators; for in area Idaho is the twelfth largest among the states.

While it is useful to face the facts in respect to representation in the Senate, it is quite useless to thunder against them. The people of the small states are naturally content. They are likewise securely protected by the constitutional proviso that their equality of representation shall not be reduced except by their own individual consents.

THE REPRESENTATIVE SYSTEM

The people of the large states are supinely acquiescent. There is no movement in this country for "a reform of the second chamber". On the other hand, there are today few competent observers outside of the Senate who would be inclined to say, as Sir Henry Maine said in 1885, that the United States Senate is "the one thoroughly successful institution which has been established since the tide of modern democracy began to run."

No modern discussion of representation is complete without some mention of proportional representation. But it is difficult to discuss proportional representation intelligibly without going into the details of systems. These cannot be given here. Innumerable schemes have been proposed. Many varieties have been put into operation. Nearly all of the countries of continental Europe have since the War gone the way of this general proposal with one or another plan. Great Britain hesitates on the precipice. Aside from electing the councils of a few cities by the proportional method, the United States is, for better or for worse, quite back-numbered, quite old-fashioned.

Briefly and inadequately described, proportional representation requires that three or more representatives shall be chosen from a district. Un-

Proportional Representation

der the so-called list system, which with many variations is applied on the continent, the voter casts his ballot primarily for this or that party list rather than for any particular candidate or candidates. Under the so-called Hare system, or single transferable vote, which is used in Ireland in certain outlying British possessions, and in a number of American and Canadian cities, the elector expresses his preferences as among candidates instead of voting for any party as such. If any group of voters actually constitute and act as a party, they indicate this fact by voting preferentially for candidates who they know are standing for their party. But this system also enables a group of voters to unite upon one or more candidates although the group may not be in any strict sense a permanent or even a transient political party. Thus the Hare system is more elastic than the list system. In each case, however, the ultimate purpose is to enable any substantial group in the multiple-member district to elect one or more representatives in proportion to the size of the group. How this is accomplished under either system cannot be explained here. The mathematics is somewhat complicated even though it rises no higher than the plane of common fractions, and even

THE REPRESENTATIVE SYSTEM

though the principle involved is crystal clear and the tasks of both the voter and the tabulator of results are relatively simple.

The logic of proportional representation depends upon the soundness of some of the common assumptions of politics. It is usually assumed that the voters are divided, or would divide if possible, into two or more relatively permanent party groups. It is assumed that this division is spontaneous, rational, and real. It is assumed, as has been said, that the representative is chosen to reflect the opinions and beliefs of those who elect him. It is assumed that a group of representatives of like-minded voting groups forming parts of the populations of the several election districts, will jointly reflect the opinions and beliefs of the nation-wide group, if such it be. It is assumed that a majority of the assembly consisting of one or more such groups of representatives, will carry out the will of a majority of the voters.

Such are some of our common assumptions. Of course they are valid in no absolute sense. Some of them are sometimes quite false to the facts. The quality of permanence in political parties does not rest wholly upon common opinions and beliefs. It is not founded exclusively in rationalized conviction. It has numerous bases—the inertia of tradition, the habit of conforming, the absence of vital differences between parties, the recognition given to existing parties by statute, and perhaps above all the existence and activity of established organization. The sheer fact of organization can sometimes preserve the breath of life in a party that is hopelessly moribund intellectually. Even so, it may be urged that, whatever the nature of party deficiencies, whatever the gap between theory and reality, whatever the lack of a cohering agency of genuine significance, parties such as they are should be represented proportionately to their numerical strengths. Theoretically this argument cannot be rebutted. But practically proportional representation is not a matter of great importance unless the parties themselves represent divisions of the voters that are of great importance. If the Democratic and Republican parties remained unaffected by the change, the election of Congressmen by this system would probably have no striking effect upon our politics.

But would these major parties survive the introduction of the system? Whether they would or not is wholly conjectural. Experience in other countries furnishes little basis for prophecy. Multiple close-knit parties prevailed practically everywhere in Europe prior to the application of the plan. It has never been tried in any sizeable country with two major parties. This may be said, however: if the break-up of the two parties followed, if a number of minor parties supplanted them, this would go far toward demonstrating the artificiality of their being—if indeed demonstration were necessary. Even so, loosely held together as the membership of our two great parties is, it may well be that the ultimate governmental result is preferable to that which would issue from a rigid crystallization of differences—and especially of sectional differences—in separately organized minor political parties. Moreover, it should not be forgotten that the election of a national party leader in the person of the President is a factor that would weigh heavily against the possible disintegration of the major parties.

There are those, like Mr. Ostrogorski, who are of the opinion that permanent political parties have ceased to be serviceable. They "should give place to special organizations, limited to particular objects and forming and reforming spontaneously, so to speak, according to the changing problems of life and the play of opinion brought about thereby." Proportional representation under the Hare system would lend itself admirably to such a new political order. But the fact is that more or less permanent political parties exist practically everywhere, and they are not likely to "give place to special organizations" at the wave of any critic's magic wand. Furthermore, it is open to grave question whether an assembly sprung from numerous impermanent and shifting special organizations would be aught but a babel of tongues.

Congress has constitutional power to regulate the manner of holding elections for senators and representatives. Congress may, therefore, at any time require that congressmen be elected by this or that scheme of proportional representation. Apparently, however, there is little if any present disposition to that end.

Consent of the Governed

It was said above that one of the common assumptions of politics is that a majority of a representative assembly will carry out the will of a majority of the voters. "Democracy," wrote Lord Bryce in 1920, "really means nothing more nor less than the rule of the whole people expressing their sovereign will by their votes." It is curious that so skilled an anatomist of bodies politic should voice such an exaggerated, not to say fanciful,

THE REPRESENTATIVE SYSTEM

view of the functional activities of such bodies. Beyond a doubt democracy means nothing more than the learned lord said; but equally beyond a doubt it means in actual operation vastly less.

The fact is that there are relatively few legislative acts in which the public is widely, positively, and vitally interested. In respect of innumerable actions taken by our legislative assemblies there is no "will of a majority", no "sovereign will", to be expressed. Countless laws are the product of the positive opinion of no more than a minority of the people. Sometimes this is a very small though it may be a very busy and relentless minority. Often there is also an oppositional minority, although organizations for opposition are seldom as effective as the organizations for offense. "All government," said Edmund Burke, "is founded on compromise and barter." But more frequently than not a large majority of the public stand ignorantly or indifferently or at least unaffirmatively by while the compromise and barter are in process. And the ultimate enactment of the law does not usually alter this apathetic attitude.

It is often said that a law cannot be enforced unless it has behind it the positive support of something like a majority public opinion. There is

THE LIVING CONSTITUTION

large fallacy in this. Whether it be true or not depends upon the subject of the law and the extent of popular interest in it. In economic legislation, for example, it would be foolish to say that the law of 1913 establishing the Federal Reserve System was supported by the approval of the many. Not one in a thousand understood a jot of its complicated purport. To take a random example in the field of social legislation, it can scarcely be said that the federal law excluding prize fight films from interstate commerce was widely championed. Yet there was no difficulty in enforcing the law whenever officials were minded to enforce it. Mr. Harold Laski grossly overstates the case when he announces that "there is no sanction for law other than the consent of the human mind." "Consent" implies a wilful allowance or acceptance. As to a large number of laws the human mind of the public at large is merely non-resistant.

Moreover, contrary to common belief, the favorable attitude of a mathematical majority is no test of whether a law can be enforced or not. The people of the Southern states, who have largely nullified the fifteenth amendment guaranteeing the vote to Negroes, are a minority of the total population. It is nevertheless doubtful whether that

THE REPRESENTATIVE SYSTEM

amendment could be enforced in those states in spirit and letter by anything short of physical force, which no government in its senses would dream of applying. It may or may not be that national prohibition is approved by an absolute majority of the people of the country. But whether it is or not has nothing whatever to do with the difficulty of enforcement. Those who disapprove are at least sufficiently numerous and sufficiently active in their opposition to create the problem that exists. Mr. G. Lowes Dickinson has aptly said: "It is not true, and it never has been and never will be true, that the majority have either the right or the power to do anything they choose, in defiance of the claims or the wishes of the minority." Wherever there is obstinate opposition by a substantial minority that is not too widely dispersed to lose effectiveness, adequate enforcement of the will of even an absolute majority becomes not merely difficult; it becomes impossible.

The "consent of the governed", therefore, means both more and less than it is usually taken to mean. If a strong minority is determined in opposition, it may mean the consent of much more than a mere head-counted majority. In such circumstances force cannot safely and successfully be

THE LIVING CONSTITUTION

applied by the majority, whatever may be the theory of the law. But as to many—perhaps most—acts of government "consent of the governed" means less than active agreement. It means little more than passive non-resistance. A vast majority of the public have little knowledge of the existence, not to mention the content, of a vast majority of the laws.

Viewed in operation, then, representative government is an ideal toward which we strive rather than a perfection which we realize. It is, so to say, less a day by day experience than an emergency device by which that powerful but intangible and amorphous being Public Opinion can, when it exists and when it wills, have its way. "Where there is a will there is a way." But in democracies there is also often a way where there is no will—of the majority.

Chapter VII

Judicial Control

THE power of the courts to declare statutes void is no new subject in these pages. It has been repeatedly referred to. In any discussion of the American constitutional system that is inevitable. It is the capstone feature of the entire system. Hardly any aspect of our institutional life is wholly free from its shadow. Hardly any piece of important legislation escapes running its gauntlet. It is America's unique contribution to the science of politics. It is a subject of never-ending discussion and appraisal—now laudatory, now condemnatory.

It is truly astonishing that this main feature crept into our system by something of stealth. The power had been exercised by one or two state courts prior to 1787. It was mooted in the famous federal convention of that year. A number of the more influential members assumed that it was implicit in the general "judicial power" which the constitution vested in the courts. The opponents of

Origin of Judicial Control

this view—and such there were—were singularly silent, as Mr. Charles Austin Beard has pointed out. Nevertheless, when all is said, this was not an ancient and established power of English and American courts. It was not comparable in status, for example, to the power to punish for contempt or to award execution of judgment. It was distinctly novel; and the few instances of its exercise by state courts in the seventeen-eighties had met with storms of local protest.

In these circumstances, if the convention entertained positive intentions in the matter, it is passing strange that they did not express these intentions in unmistakable words. No proposal to that end was brought forward. There was in consequence no real for-and-against debate on the subject. Nor has it been shown that the inexplicit muteness of the constitution as to this matter was born of a deliberate purpose to avoid specific commitment upon a delicate and highly controversial subject. It is at least possible, not to say probable, that, whatever individual members of the convention thought about judicial review, they did not see with the vision of other-worldly prophets the vast institutional consequence of the exercise or non-exercise of this power, as the case might be.

JUDICIAL CONTROL

At any rate, whether intentionally or inadvertently, it was left to the courts (and especially, as events proved, to Chief Justice John Marshall) to assert this great power by implication. This has often been called judicial "usurpation". In the very year of the making of the constitution Richard D. Spaight, a member of the convention, so characterized the exercise of this power by the courts of his own state, North Carolina. And critics continue to this day to hurl with fire and fury this charge of usurpation.

The word is mischosen. The possibility of the exercise of this power by the courts was of a certainty in the air at the time the constitution was framed. To be sure, the power was not expressly granted to the courts; but, by the same testimony, it was not denied or limited. Nor was it lodged elsewhere. Congress and the states were not expressly authorized to be the final judges of their own constitutional competence, which they would have been in the absence of judicial review. The most that can be said is that the courts seized upon a power which they might have abjured and which was not unmistakably vested in any one branch of the government. Moreover, their legal right to do this could be sustained by arguments which, even

THE LIVING CONSTITUTION

though not wholly unanswerable, were assuredly not wholly illogical. This cannot properly be characterized as usurpation. Even if it could be the lapse of more than a century should be sufficient to quiet the title of the veriest of usurpers. Had we been so minded, the "usurper" could have been ousted long since from the throne.

Marshall's View — The authority of the courts to declare void an act of Congress was in 1803 laid down by the Supreme Court in the famous case of Marbury v. Madison. The argument of Marshall may be briefed by quoting a few of his own words: The constitution is a "superior paramount law." A "legislative act, contrary to the constitution, is not law;" it is void. "If two laws conflict with each other, the courts must decide on the operation of each. So, if a law be in opposition to the constitution," the determination of which of these governs "is of the very essence of judicial duty." The constitution, being "superior to any ordinary act of the legislature, . . . must govern the case to which they both apply." Those who controvert this principle "would subvert the very foundation of all written constitutions." In these few sentences lies the whole of the logic of judicial review.

JUDICIAL CONTROL

It is not irrefutable logic. It is true that courts cannot apply both of two conflicting laws. Imperatively one or the other must give way. This is the pivot of Marshall's argument. But the general rule is that the later in point of enactment controls. Marshall here altered this rule out of hand. He substituted "superior" for "later". Such a substitution was not wholly unreasonable. But neither would it have been unreasonable to apply the general rule. The paramountcy of the constitution may be conceded; but the nub question is: who shall determine what the constitution means? Why should it be assumed that Congress, the maker of the laws, has any less intelligence concerning the meaning of legal words or has any less respect for or willingness to abide by the prescriptions of the fundamental law than have the courts?

"To what purpose are powers limited," asked the great Chief Justice in this case, "and to what purpose is that limitation committed to writing, if these limits may, at any time, be passed by those intended to be restrained?" With equal propriety might the Court have addressed this question in respect of the power it was at the moment exercising, the power of judicial review. The Court was and is, no less than Congress, an organ of limited powers. Indeed in that very case, to defeat a provision of law enacted by Congress, the Court applied a provision of the constitution which was held by strained construction to impose a limitation upon its own original jurisdiction. But what authority is there beyond the Court itself to prevent it from passing the constitutional limits imposed upon it? None whatever. To what purpose then, it might be retorted, are its powers limited by written words, "if these limits may, at any time, be passed by those intended to be restrained?"

The chief implied restriction put upon the courts by the constitution is that they may be vested only with judicial power. Did this judicial power include the right of veto? To determine which of two conflicting laws governs may be the "very essence of judicial duty"; but to resolve this difficulty in a particular way, to resolve it not by reference to the dates of enactment, but by nullifying the later statute because of its inferiority to the earlier constitution was not an essentially inherent and generally accepted element of judicial power. Moreover, the history of many countries refutes the notion that to deny this power to the courts "would subvert the very foundation of all written constitutions."

JUDICIAL CONTROL

Such is the law, however; such is the basis of the much-discussed doctrine of judicial review.

As applicable to acts of Congress its results are difficult to estimate. After the trivial act involved in the Marbury case no statute of Congress was held invalid until 1857—a period of fifty-four years. Decision was then rendered in the history-making case of Dred Scott v. Sanford. Mr. Albert J. Beveridge says in his *Life of John Marshall* that "but for Marbury v. Madison, the power of the Supreme Court to annul acts of Congress probably would not have been insisted upon thereafter;" for "nearly seventy years would have passed without any question arising as to the omnipotence of Congress." This is an extraordinary view. The power to annul acts of Congress does not depend upon the frequency of its exercise but upon the recurrence and vigor of its assertion. At the very same term of court in 1803 this power was "insisted upon" in a much more important case involving the constitutionality of the Judiciary Act of 1802. That the law was upheld is neither here nor there. There would have been no case at all had not the Court had power to declare it void. In 1819—to cite only one other case—decision was reached in the important case of McCulloch

Applied to Acts of Congress

v. Maryland. One of the two main points "insisted upon" was that Congress had no power to charter the Bank of the United States. The Court sustained the power. In a notable opinion Marshall expounded the doctrine of liberal construction of the powers of the federal government. His logic was unanswerable; benefit to the country was everlasting. Other instances might be mentioned in which questions "as to the omnipotence of Congress" were raised in the Supreme Court prior to 1857. The mere fact that such questions were considered, even though the answer was favorable to the exerted powers of Congress, was an emphatic assertion of the power of the courts to annul statutes. The authority being thus established and kept alive by repetitious iteration, the sooner or later exercise of the judicial veto was inevitable.

In all, however, only fifty-three acts of Congress or parts of acts have been declared void. Slightly more than half of these annulments have fallen in the last twenty-five years. Most of the half a hundred were of relatively minor or at least of fugitive significance. Not more than six or seven have been of first-rate consequence. The issue involved in the Dred Scott case was effaced by the Civil War and the resulting abolition of slavery.

JUDICIAL CONTROL

In 1871 it was held that Congress was without power to impose taxes on income derived from state and local governments. Hence the salaries paid by these units are free from federal taxation. Similarly exempt is the income derived from state and municipal bonds. In 1895 a federal income tax law was declared void; and not until 1913 was the power to enact such a law restored to Congress by the sixteenth amendment. In 1883 in the Civil Rights Cases the Supreme Court laid down the rule that the fourteenth amendment gave Congress no authority to legislate affirmatively in respect to private rights. The statute was void, therefore, which required that colored persons be given "the same accommodations and privileges in all inns, public conveyances, and places of amusement as are enjoyed by white citizens". Wholly apart from the particular act that was voided, this rule of construction was one of the most important ever uttered by the Court. A contrary interpretation would have so expanded the power of Congress as to make at least possible a virtual destruction of the federal division of powers.

In recent years the most significant congressional laws that have met defeat by the Court have been concerned with labor. The federal Employer's Liability Act had to be amended to meet the views of the Court as to its original unconstitutional scope. In the same year, 1908, the law was annulled which prohibited railroads from discriminating against employees because of membership in labor unions. In 1918 and again in 1922 federal child labor laws succumbed. In 1923 the minimum wage law applicable to the District of Columbia was interdicted.

The latest congressional acts voided were those, previously mentioned, which impose restrictions upon the President's power of removal.

Over against this relatively small number of important laws that have been judicially vetoed must be set the much larger number—well over two hundred and fifty—which the Court, being urged, has refused to nullify. Many of these have been supremely significant. The list is too formidable to be given here. Suffice it to say that almost every important congressional act upon any new subject or new phase of an old subject is challenged as to its constitutionality.

It has already been pointed out, however, that the complete effect of judicial review is immeasurable. It certainly is not revealed by mere statistics of laws annulled and laws sustained. For no

JUDICIAL CONTROL

one can say what laws might have been enacted by Congress had the Supreme Court never assumed the role of a council of censors.

In a speech delivered in 1913 Mr. Justice Holmes said: "I do not think the United States would come to an end if we lost our power to declare an act of Congress void. I do think the Union would be imperiled if we could not make that declaration as to the laws of the several states. For one in my place sees how often a local policy prevails with those who are not trained to national views and how often action is taken that embodies what the commerce clause was meant to end."

Applied to State Acts

There is certainly a valid distinction between the one and the other exercise of this power. There are reasons inherent in our federalism why this power in respect of acts of Congress is of less importance than it is in respect of acts of the states. To a limited extent judicial review has served to protect the states against encroachment by Congress. To a much larger extent has it served to protect the exercise of national power against invasion by the states. Manifestly to protect the integrity of national power is of greater importance than to preserve the powers of states inviolate, though there have been states' rights men from Thomas

Jefferson to Albert C. Ritchie who have disputed this proposition. It is difficult to see how the states could have been held in constitutional rein unless some central agency had been endowed with competence to apply the brakes. Disallowance of state acts by Congress would certainly have been less satisfactory than by the courts. John C. Calhoun's proposal to submit constitutional amendments in case of disagreement between a state and the national government in respect to the division or scope of powers was put forward primarily to the end of holding Congress in check. In any case, however superbly logical, his proposal was likewise superbly impractical.

Of course the exercise of federal judicial control over the states is not confined to the annulment of acts that are held to impair the federal division by trespass upon the powers of the nation. Indeed the power is exerted far more frequently upon acts that have nothing to do with the federal division. The federal principle is in no wise involved, for example, in the provision which prohibits the states from passing laws impairing the obligation of contracts. It was deemed wise to place this restriction upon the states quite irrespective of what powers were given to Congress. Precisely the same

JUDICIAL CONTROL

thing is true of the prohibition against a deprivation of life, liberty, or property without due process of law or a denial of the equal protection of the laws. On the other hand, when the courts prevent the states from taxing or otherwise interfering with interstate or foreign commerce or some instrumentality of the national government, the power of judicial review is used to protect federal powers from invasion.

Whatever may have been the intention of the framers of the constitution as to statutes of Congress, fairly strong evidence of their intention to have the federal courts pass upon the constitutionality of state laws is found in the famous twenty-fifth section of the Judiciary Act of 1789. This was enacted by the First Congress, which contained a number of members of the Convention of 1787. It expressly provided that whenever a state court upheld a state law which was alleged to be in conflict with the national constitution, the case might be carried to the United States Supreme Court. Congressional authorization of judicial review of state acts thus existed from the beginning of our constitutional history.

In the course of time, however, it transpired that reactionary state courts were often far more zealous to declare progressive state laws void than was the Supreme Court. They did this by applying the guaranties of the federal constitution, and especially the guaranties in behalf of property rights. After years of somewhat bitter agitation Congress provided in 1914 that cases might be carried to the Supreme Court even where the decision of the state court was in support of the right claimed under the national constitution. In other words, judicial review by the Supreme Court was to be used as a buffer between state legislatures and their own courts. It was no longer to be employed solely to prevent state legislatures from violating the constitution; it was now to be used to prevent state courts from upsetting their own state laws by applying alleged federal rights too strictly.

Veto by State Courts

Such cases can be carried up, however, only upon a writ of certiorari. The entire Supreme Court has to pass upon the granting of this writ. It is not, therefore, easily secured—not nearly so easily as a writ of error, which is granted by a single judge or even by the clerk of the Court. It is this latter writ that is used when the state court denies the federal right and upholds the state law. Judged by the number of cases in which certiorari has been granted, the law of 1914 has not met the

JUDICIAL CONTROL

expectations of its sponsors. It is quite impossible, however, to tell what disciplinary effect its mere existence has had upon some of our more hard-minded state judges.

More than a thousand state acts have been reviewed by the highest court of the land. About one out of every four has been invalidated. The vast majority of these have fallen under the hammer of the contract clause, the commerce clause, or the due process and equal protection clauses. In the progress of time the first of these has decreased in importance, while the second and third have steadily increased.

Among cases which never reached the Supreme Court, no computation has ever been made of the number of state laws that have been struck down by the state courts and the lower federal courts because of declared conflict with the federal constitution. The number certainly runs into thousands. The rebound of such decisions, however, is not comparable to that which a Supreme Court pronouncement sometimes carries. For instance, in 1919 the Arizona employers' liability law was saved by a hair—almost, one might say, by the absence of a hair. The Court divided four to four, there being one vacancy at the time. A law can be either sustained or annulled by an even vote. That depends upon what the judgment of the court below was. For such a vote merely operates to let the lower judgment stand. In the case involving this particular law the decisions of the lower courts both state and federal had been favorable to the law. A similar vote on the Oregon minimum wage law had the effect of defeating the law, for the judgment of the lower court had been against its validity. The point is, however, that if the opinion of the lower courts on the Arizona liability law had been unfavorable, or if, being favorable, there had been a bare majority of the Supreme Court against it, the final word upon the subject by that tribunal would have inferentially voided workmen's compensation laws of like character in many other states of the Union.

The fact has been mentioned that the repercussion of Supreme Court decisions is not always complete. States sometimes go on enforcing a law after the Court has declared a similar law in some other state invalid. Indeed, so far as the strictly legal effect of any such decision is concerned, the very state whose law is declared void may perversely continue to carry it into execution until it has compelled every ultimate person who objects

JUDICIAL CONTROL

to it to push his cause to the highest court and secure a judgment specifically protecting *him* from its operation. But this would be arrantly senseless and wholly unfair to litigants in the matter of trouble and expense. A law once declared void is commonly regarded as completely dead. And the killing of a law for one state is usually followed by a cessation of the enforcement of similar laws, if any, in other states. Occasionally, therefore, a judgment by the Supreme Court reaches further than appears upon its face.

Apart from decisions on federal questions, state courts also void many laws because of conflict with provisions of state constitutions which have no relation to national limitations imposed upon the states. Judicial review permeates our entire jurisprudential system. It runs the whole gamut—from an ordinance of some petty city council that is held to conflict with the city's fundamental law, its charter, to a law of Congress that is declared to be counter to the highest of all in our hierarchy of fundamental laws. It lurks at the door of every legislative chamber. It is all-pervasive. It is, if not omniscient, at any rate omniprevalent. Which is not to imply that every unconstitutional law is judicially sentenced to death. No doubt many laws are being enforced which might be annulled if the point of unconstitutionality were seen and adequately argued before the courts. Many members of the legal profession are curiously unalert to constitutional questions, despite the prominence of these questions in our system of laws. The marvel is that so many flimsy points are pressed before the courts and that settled principles of construction, while frequently rehashed to no useful purpose, are not always pushed to their logical conclusion in application to novel laws and circumstances. "The life of the law has not been its logic," says Mr. Justice Holmes. Of judicial review of state acts this is peculiarly apt.

Judicial Veto in History
Writing in 1912 Mr. Horace A. Davis said: "It is only recently that" the situation arising out of judicial review "has attracted public attention and become the subject of political criticism." Nothing could be more awry with the facts. It drew public attention and evoked lively criticism almost from the beginning. It is true that Marbury v. Madison received little contemporaneous notice. The provision of law that was voided in that case was of paltry significance; and political interest in the case had, before it was decided, been swallowed up in larger issues. But beginning with Fletcher

JUDICIAL CONTROL

v. Peck, the famous Georgia land fraud case decided in 1810, vigorously voiced opposition to the exercise of this power by the courts has been recrudescent down to the present day.

It should be remarked, however, that in nearly every instance those who reprobated the power were prompted by their antagonism to the effect of its exercise in this or that particular case. Mr. Charles Warren has properly pointed out that "the history of the years succeeding 1800 clearly shows that, with regard to this judicial function, the political parties divided not on lines of general theory of government, or of constitutional law, or of Nationalism against Localism, but on lines of political, social or economic interest." It would not be difficult, moreover, to prove a considerable amount of inconsistency on the part of some of the critics of judicial review. For, as Webster remarked as early as 1826, the successive efforts to shake the public confidence in the decisions of the Supreme Court "have found those who were, at one time, its enemies, at another, its friends." Throughout our history judicial control has been loved or hated according as its concrete results have from time to time been approved or disapproved.

It is unnecessary to review here the numerous

instances in which nullification of laws by the courts, and especially by the Supreme Court, has met with local or widespread denunciation. In rare instances there has even been official attempt by one state or another defiantly to nullify such nullification by ignoring the solemnly pronounced orders of the Court. On these occasions of passionate protest it often befell that the whole institution of judicial control was vehemently execrated.

Recent Attacks The year 1895 may probably be said to mark the beginning of the more recent attacks upon this power in the courts. In that year unpopular decisions were rendered in three important cases. In an effort to reach some of the evils of "big business" Congress had in 1890 enacted the Sherman Anti-Trust Act. The first case under this law to reach the Supreme Court was the United States v. E. C. Knight Company. The opinion of the Court appeared to draw the teeth of the law. In point of fact the case was abominably presented to the courts by the Department of Justice. The Court was far less responsible than the law officers of the government for the decision that was reached. In any event, there was here no question of judicial veto of the law but merely a judicial determination of what the statute meant.

JUDICIAL CONTROL

In Pollock v. Farmers' Loan & Trust Company the federal income tax law of 1894 was held void, at least in part. Politically and economically speaking there was here involved a sectional issue. The financiers of the East applauded. It was they whom the measure oppressed. The agrarians of the South and West stormed.

The case of Eugene Debs, decided in the same year, first raised prominently the issue of what came to be known as "government by injunction". In the summer of 1894 there was a great railway strike in Chicago. An injunction was issued by a lower United States Court commanding Debs and three other officers of the American Railway Union "and all other persons combining or conspiring with them" to desist from doing certain generally described acts which prevented the operation of trains carrying interstate commerce and the mails. The authority to issue this injunction and to jail those who disobeyed it was sustained by the Supreme Court. Here again was no question of the power of the Court to invalidate laws. But incensed people do not make fine distinctions between one and another unloved exercise of judicial or any other kind of power.

The closing years of the old and the opening

THE LIVING CONSTITUTION

years of the new century witnessed an increasingly narrow application of constitutional inhibitions upon social and labor legislation by some of the state courts. Statute after statute was purged from the books by judicial pronouncement. The Supreme Court, by reason of one or two unfortunate decisions, came in for far larger opprobrium than was its just desert. Lochner v. New York, which annulled an eight hour law for bakeries, became almost a symbol of judicial tyranny. Decision in that case was handed down in 1905. In the decade that followed there was a steady stream of articles and books attacking and defending judicial review as an institution. In politics the movement for curbing this power reached its pinnacle in the campaign of 1912, when the Progressive party led by Mr. Roosevelt boldly advocated a foolish reform known as the recall of judicial decisions. A number of states provided for the recall of judges as well as other officers. Latterly the agitation has somewhat subsided; but it has by no means wholly ceased. Nor is it likely to die utterly.

Reform Proposals — From time to time a great variety of proposals have been made for abolishing or modifying judicial review. John Marshall himself, though not publicly, made one of the earliest and likewise

[258]

JUDICIAL CONTROL

one of the most drastic suggestions. On the eve of the impeachment trial of Judge Samuel Chase in 1806 he wrote privately to that irascible old Bourbon, then under fire: "I think the modern doctrine of impeachment should yield to an appellate jurisdiction in the legislature. A reversal of those opinions deemed unsound by the legislature would certainly better comport with the mildness of our character than would a removal of the judge who has rendered them unknowing his fault."

Extraordinary proposal! Let the courts say to the legislature, "Your law is unconstitutional." Let the legislature retort, "It is not." Judicial veto would be merely pious admonition, a shaking of the finger. But as Mr. Beveridge has pointed out, the great Chief Justice was at the moment seriously alarmed over the fate of judges, himself included, who might be arraigned at the bar of the Senate in impeachment proceedings.

Abolish the whole system of review of state acts by the Supreme Court, voted the Virginia Assembly in 1821. And the fire-eating chief justice of the state, Spencer Roane, drafted a proposed amendment to that end. Let every justice be compelled to write his own opinion, wrote Thomas Jefferson about the same time; let Congress denounce; then if a judge fails to mend his ways, let impeachment follow. Another extraordinary proposal! As if a judicial opinion disapproved by Congress constituted the "treason, bribery, or other high crimes and misdemeanors" for which judges may be constitutionally impeached! Later he advocated the much milder proposal of limiting the terms of judges to four or six years.

When the laws of a state are questioned let the Senate have appellate jurisdiction, urged Senator Richard M. Johnson of Kentucky in 1821. Repeal the odious twenty-fifth section of the Judiciary Act, implored Congressman Stevenson of Virginia a year later. Require unanimous concurrence of the judges to invalidate a state law, said Senator Johnson, returning to the attack in 1823. Require five out of seven votes, proposed the Senate Judiciary Committee a year later; and even Daniel Webster seemed at one time not wholly oppositional to this. Repeal the twenty-fifth section, said the House Judiciary Committee in 1831; and the subject was thereupon furiously debated. Destroy the power branch and root, cried the Abolition press after the Dred Scott decision in 1857. "Reorganize and reinvigorate" the Supreme Court, shouted the Northern Republicans in 1859–60—

JUDICIAL CONTROL

which could only mean increase the number of judges on the Supreme Bench and "pack" the Court with an anti-slavery majority.

During Johnson's administration rumors were rife that the Supreme Court would declare the Reconstruction Acts void. In this emergency the House actually passed a bill by a large majority requiring a two-thirds vote of the Court to invalidate an act of Congress; but the Senate did not act upon it. Bills were likewise introduced in both houses withdrawing from the Court jurisdiction over cases arising under these particular acts.

And so from age to age, with each new outbreak of protest over some hated exercise of judicial veto, the changes have been rung upon suggestions for bridling the power of the courts. Popular election of federal judges for limited terms has been many times put forward, in complete disregard of the fact that this method of choice has produced some of the most reactionary of state courts.

Perhaps the most persistent of all proposals has been for the requirement of an extraordinary majority vote to invalidate a law. One or two states have already laid this imposition upon their highest courts; and it is recurrently urged for application to the Supreme Court. Five to four decisions

Five to Four Decisions

upon laws that enlist wide interest furnish a specially alluring target for fire. Truth to speak, such decisions do not differ in essence from any other governmental action that is reached by an inconsequential majority. But the smallness of the number of the judges accentuates the scantness of the margin. It seems almost like coin-tossing. One change of personnel and a lost law would be saved. Not wholly unnaturally it arouses ill-feeling and provokes animadversion.

Judges are wont to say, when about to wield the judicial axe, that this is an awful, a solemn, power, never to be exercised in case of doubt; any uncertainty must be resolved in favor of the validity of the law. And it sometimes seems that, the closer the division among the judges themselves, the more earnest is the headsman majority to assert this backward-leaning attitude of approach to the question in hand. No doubt most of us seek to appease and justify ourselves. That is a fortunate human failing. But in judicial opinions the result, starkly looked at, is sometimes humorous. Take the instance of Mr. Justice Sutherland who in 1923 spoke for the majority of five who held that minimum wage legislation was void. Weapon in hand he mounted the scaffold with the assertion that

JUDICIAL CONTROL

"every possible presumption is in favor of the validity of an act of Congress until overcome beyond rational doubt." He then proceeded to slay the statute. But three of his colleagues, Chief Justice Taft and Mr. Justices Sanford and Holmes, dissented; while a fourth, Mr. Justice Brandeis, who had some years before argued with consummate ability to sustain the constitutionality of such legislation, refrained from participating in the case. Did the learned justice mean to imply that four of his colleagues, who entertained not only doubts but also quite positive disagreement with his views, were irrational? Did he mean to say that their hard-held and forcibly stated convictions on the subject did not present even a "possible presumption" in favor of the validity of the act? It is less difficult to be patient with such assertions of reluctant attitude than it is to take them seriously. They are in fact quite meaningless.

Few of the advocates of an extraordinary majority vote seem to realize that the Supreme Court has the power to render such a requirement completely ineffective. If the members of the Court believe that decisions should be reached by an ordinary majority, they have only to agree among themselves that, in the event of a five to four divi-

[263]

sion, a sufficient number of the minority will record themselves with the majority in order to meet the requirement of the law. Contrary to popular impression it is highly probable that disagreeing judges do not always put themselves specifically upon the record as dissenters.

Contempt of Court — Every court must have the power of self-preservation. It must have the power summarily to quell an obstructing disturbance in or near the courtroom. It must have the power to compel a witness to give the testimony demanded of him or to prevent a witness from insulting the court. Every court must also be able to enforce obedience outside of the court to certain writs, processes, and decrees. It must be able, for example, to compel an absent witness to attend and to enforce any order that it issues after the due trial of a case. Clearly such powers as these inhere in any general grant of "judicial power" that is worthy the name. They derive from common-sense. Courts must be competent to carry on with their business in orderly fashion and to make their judgments effective. From time immemorial the power to commit for contempt has been employed for these purposes. The offender enjoys no right to be tried by a jury. In fact he is not really tried at all. Unless he purges

JUDICIAL CONTROL

himself of his contempt he is abruptly remanded to jail. And quite properly.

With the growing industrialization of the country and the organization of labor unions, disputes between employers and employees became more and more frequent. There were strikes and there were lockouts. One of the practises pursued by the employers in such emergencies was to go into a court of equity, especially if possible a lower United States court, and ask for an injunction to restrain the strikers or those locked out from doing this, that, and the other thing. If the injunction issued, and if its orders were thereafter disobeyed, the offenders were haled into court and were promptly imprisoned for contempt.

For years there has been widespread agitation against this use of the injunction and exercise of the power to commit for contempt. It is said to be grossly abusive; and such it often is. Three main objections are raised. First, these injunctions are sometimes of a blanket variety. They impose a restraining order upon persons who were not specifically named at all. The above-mentioned Debs injunction ran not only against Debs and three other named officers of the union but also against "all other persons combining or conspiring with

Government by Injunction

[265]

them." This was extraordinary. It was at least conceivable that a person might be punished for disobeying an order that he had never heard of.

Second, these injunctions are often enormously complicated and in spite of their voluminousness are as to some inhibitions extremely indefinite. As District Judge Amidon said in 1923: "During the 30 years that courts have been dealing with strikes by means of injunctions, these orders have steadily grown in length, complexity, and the vehemence of their rhetoric. They are full of the rich vocabulary of synonyms which is a part of our English language. They are also replete with superlative words and the superlative phrases of which the legal mind is fond. The result is that such writs have steadily become more and more complex and prolix. All of this, it seems to me, is foreign to their legitimate purpose. They, like the proper bill in such cases, ought to arise out of the facts of each specific case. Injunctions are addressed to laymen. They ought to be so brief and plain that laymen can understand them. They ought to be framed in the fewest possible words. The order should not express the bias or violence of a party to such a controversy or his attorney." The injunction issued in the Debs case in 1894 was amply vague and com-

JUDICIAL CONTROL

prehensive. But Mr. Felix Frankfurter and Mr. James Landis have by a striking parallel shown how mild and specific it was in comparison with that issued by District Judge Wilkerson in the Railroad Shop Crafts case in 1922. There has been, they say, "steady extension from carefully limited injunctions in the earlier days to sweeping orders granted almost *pro forma.*"

Third, and perhaps most important of all, these injunctions invariably prohibit certain acts which are also offenses under the criminal laws. If, for instance, during an industrial controversy, assault is committed or property is damaged or destroyed, these acts are nearly always not only breaches of the injunction; they are also crimes. But the perpetrators can be summoned before the judge who issued the injunction and, without any formal indictment or trial by jury, can be summarily remanded to jail for contempt.

From the time of the Debs case on, there was constant agitation in and out of Congress for a law that would place some restriction upon the power of the courts in this matter. The movement, so far as the power of federal courts is concerned, finally fructified in the Clayton Act of 1914. This act provided that the accused might demand a jury

Clayton Act

[267]

trial in any case involving disobedience to a writ or decree of a lower United States court, provided the act done was of such character as to constitute also a criminal offense either under federal or state law. It was scrupulously provided, that this should not apply to "contempts committed in the presence of the court, or so near thereto as to obstruct the administration of justice, nor to contempts committed in disobedience of any lawful writ, process, order, rule, decree, or command entered in any suit or action brought or prosecuted in the name of, or on behalf of the United States." The authority of the courts to exercise summary power where such power is manifestly indispensable was thus carefully preserved. Moreover, the right of jury trial was limited to those cases in which the disobedience is to an injunction sought and obtained at the behest of a private person—that is, in labor cases, the aggrieved employer. It cannot be invoked where the disobedience is to an order issued in connection with a suit brought by the government itself.

In 1925 this law was upheld by the Supreme Court. Certain striking employees of a railroad had been enjoined, at the request of the company, from combining and conspiring to interfere with

JUDICIAL CONTROL

interstate commerce by picketing and using force and violence. Contempt proceedings followed. The employees demanded trial by jury. The District Court refused on the ground that the Clayton act was unconstitutional. This decision the Supreme Court reversed. A criminal contempt, said the Court, is fundamentally the same as a criminal case. "The proceeding is not between the parties to the original suit, but between the public and the defendant." In a criminal case the accused has a constitutional right to be tried by jury. Why should he not be given the same right in a class of contempts which are properly described as "criminal offenses"? Whether from the viewpoint of the history of punishment for contempt or from the viewpoint of common sense, it is difficult to see how any other conclusion could have been reached. Thus was settled at least one important point in the long battle against "government by injunction".

Criticism of and opposition to the use of the power to commit for contempt has not been confined to cases arising out of labor disputes. As far back as 1831 harsh and tyrannical uses of the power led to the famous impeachment trial of United States District Judge James H. Peck of Missouri. He was not convicted; but Congress

Contempt Power in General

speedily enacted a law imposing limitations upon this power. It was to be exercised to punish for misbehavior only when the act in question is committed "in the presence" of the court "or so near thereto as to obstruct the administration of justice." That sounds very simple and direct. But the phrase "so near thereto" has been the stumbling block. How near must that be? If during the pendency of a trial or an appeal the rulings of a judge are criticized in newspaper editorial or in open letter, does such action as this constitute the kind of misbehavior that may be dealt with in contempt proceedings?

This statute is still unrepealed. But in 1918 it was given a most unfortunate and, it would seem, highly questionable twist by the Supreme Court. As Mr. Frankfurter and Mr. Landis have said: "Stimulated by the Toledo Newspaper Co. case, some of the lower Federal courts, wholly unmindful of the history of the Act of 1831, in effect have written this Act off the statute-books."

There are recent evidences, however, that the Supreme Court is awake to the dangers of contempt abuses. Sustaining in 1925 the power of the President to pardon persons committed for this offense, the Court wrote with fine restraint: "May

JUDICIAL CONTROL

it not be fairly said that in order to avoid possible mistake, undue prejudice, or needless severity, the chance of pardon should exist at least as much in favor of a person convicted by a judge without a jury as in favor of one convicted in a jury trial?" Only a month later, moreover, the Court reversed a contempt conviction by a lower United States judge because there had been "undue prejudice" and "needless severity". The facts need not detain us; but the Court held that "it was harsh in the circumstances to order the arrest", and "the procedure pursued was unfair and oppressive". Tyrannical use of the power to commit for contempt was not due process of law. Thus not only legislatures but also lower courts are by the Supreme Court curbed to the bit of this magic phrase—"due process".

Chapter VIII

In Conclusion

The constitution of the United States was not handed down on Mount Sinai by the Lord God of Hosts. It is not revealed law. It is no final cause. It is human means. The system of government which it provides can scarcely be read at all in the stately procession of its simple clauses. Yet its broad outlines are there sketched with deft strokes. Through long unfolding years it has been tried in the crucible of men's minds and hearts. It lacks alike perfection and perfectibility. But it has been found good—exceedingly good. It is not to be worshipped. But it is certainly to be respected. Nor is it to be lightly altered, even if that were possible. The unit that it serves or should serve is not society but the individual. As we slowly move from individualism to collectivism, as move no doubt we must, hark We the People to remember that men cannot be made good by law, that nothing that is human is infallible, and that governments, whatever their form, are only as moral as those who hold the throttle of power at the moment.

BIBLIOGRAPHICAL NOTE

Bibliographical Note

The literature bearing upon the topics discussed in this book is almost limitless. Only a few suggestions can here be made.

Among the best works generally descriptive of the entire American system of government are: Charles A. Beard, *American Government and Politics*, fourth edition, 1924; William B. Munro, *The Government of the United States*, 1919; Frederic A. Ogg and P. Orman Ray, *Introduction to American Government*, 1922; James T. Young, *The New American Government and Its Work*, second edition, 1923; James Bryce, *The American Commonwealth*, second edition, 1910.

The Federalist, published in many editions, is a series of papers by Alexander Hamilton, James Madison and John Jay, written while the ratification of the federal constitution was pending in 1787-88. Among comments on the constitution it is our foremost classic.

Robert Livingston Schuyler's *Constitution of the United States*, 1923, is probably the best historical survey of the formation of the constitution in brief compass.

J. Allen Smith's *The Spirit of American Government*, 1907, is a stimulating study of some underlying principles of our government; but the main thesis of the book is somewhat overdrawn.

Woodrow Wilson's *Constitutional Government of the United States*, 1908, is an excellent critique of the more important features of our national government. His *Congressional Government*, 1885, though somewhat out of date has not ceased to be well worth reading.

C. G. Tiedman's *The Unwritten Constitution of the United States*, 1890, is a suggestive little volume.

William MacDonald's *A New Constitution for a New America*, 1921, is a plea for a general revision of our constitutional system. It expresses views that are contrary to many of those herein set forth.

On the subject of judicial review Charles A. Beard's *The Supreme Court and the Constitution*, 1912, and Horace A. Davis's *The Judicial Veto*, 1913, present opposing views of the intentions of those who drafted and ratified the constitution. Gilbert P. Rowe attacks the system in *Our Judi-*

BIBLIOGRAPHICAL NOTE

cial Oligarchy, 1912; and J. Hampden Daugherty defends it in *The Power of the Federal Judiciary Over Legislation*, 1912.

H. L. West's *Federal Power: Its Growth and Necessity* is a vigorous defense of national centralization. Franklin Pierce's *Federal Usurpation*, 1908, denounces it.

G. B. Brown's *Leadership of Congress*, 1922, discusses the disorganized procedure of the House of Representatives. Lindsay Rogers's *The American Senate*, 1926, is a brilliant little book containing many new slants on the relation between senatorial powers and procedure and the powers of the executive.

INDEX

INDEX

Agricultural interests, over-represented in the Senate, 221-227
Amendment, of United States constitution, 19-21; of state constitutions, 21-24
Amidon, J., quoted, 266
Appointing power, see *President*
Bagehot, Walter, quoted, 16, 121, 132, 134
Bankruptcy laws, 80
Beveridge, A. J., quoted, 243
Bicameral legislatures, 162-170
Bill of rights, nature of, 72-81; necessity of, against national government, 81-83; changing character of, 113; English, 113
Bills of attainder, 74, 81, 83
Borgeaud, Charles, quoted, 9
Brandeis, J., quoted, 94
Brewer, J., quoted, 91, 113
Brougham, Lord, quoted, 38, 202, 203
Bryce, James, quoted, 9, 13, 16, 113, 152, 163, 200, 232
Bureaucracy and federalism, 64
Burke, Edmund, quoted, 203, 232
Cabinet, British, as leader of legislation, 121-125, 132-134; responsibility of, 136-140
Cabinet, President's, 26, 116; proposal to give seats in Congress, 145-149
Checks and balances, nature of, 150-153; and democracy, 154-162; under state constitutions, 199, 200; survival of, 200, 201
Child labor, laws and amendment, 160, 162
Chinese Exclusion Act, 90, 91

Civil Rights Cases, 245
Civil Service, 178
Clayton Act, injunctions under, 267-269
Commerce clause, 42-55; police powers under, 49-55
Commons, House of, distribution of seats in, 17, 218; Cabinet leadership of, 121-125; 132-134; Cabinet responsibility to, 136-140
Congress, constitutional amendments proposed by, 19, 20; power of, to alter constitution, 29; commerce power of, 42-55; and presidential leadership, 115-118
Congressional districts, see *Representation*
Consent of governed, 232-236
Constitution, United States, defined, 11; scope of, 12; customs of, 18-31; amendment of, 19-24, 35, 36; development of, 25-31; interpretation of, 33
Constitutions, definition of, 7-11; written and unwritten, 13-16; flexible and rigid, 16-25; amendment of, 19-24
Contempts of court, 264-271
Contract clause, 80, 81
Cooley, J., quoted, 8
Davis, H. A., quoted, 254
Debs Case, 257, 266, 267
Democracy, and checks and balances, 154-162
Dicey, quoted, 67
Dickinson, G. L., quoted, 235
Dred Scott Case, 243, 244, 260
Due process of law, 77-79; as applied

[281]

INDEX

to acts of Congress, 108-110; as applied to acts of the states, 110-112; in contempt cases, 271

Education, power of Congress over, 38, 39

Eighteenth amendment; see *Prohibition*

Elections, recent British, 137-140; national in the United States, 140, 141; difference between British and American, 140-142

Employers' Liability Act, 47, 48

Espionage Act, 82, 86-88

Executive power, vested in President, 114, 115; regulation of, by Congress, 118; see also *President*

Ex post facto laws, 81, 83

Farmers' bloc, 222

Federalism, definition of, 34; tendency toward centralization, 36; powers of states under, 40-55; encroachment on powers of states under, 46-55; and nationalism, 58, 59; reasons for, 60-65; and bureaucracy, 64; problem of division of powers under, 67-71

Fletcher v. Peck, 254, 255

Ford, H. J., quoted, 147, 148

Foreign affairs, leadership in, 117

Frankfurter, Felix, quoted, 267, 270

Freedom, of speech, 74, 76, 82, 84-89; of religion, 74, 83; of assembly, 74, 83; of contract, 112

Gardiner, A. G., quoted, 133

Gladstone, W. E., quoted, 13

Government, of laws and of men, 1-5; by injunction, 265-269

Grants-in-aid, 57, 58

Great Britain, unwritten constitution of, 13-15; changes in constitution of, 16-18; politics in, 18; see also *Cabinet, Commons, Lords*

Habeas corpus, 74, 81, 89-94

Hamilton, Alexander, quoted, 101, 153, 154, 157, 158

Hand, Learned, J., quoted, 86

Hare system, see *Proportional representation*

Hay, John, quoted, 195, 196

Holmes, Oliver Wendell, J., quoted, 33, 87, 88, 93, 120, 247, 254

Hours of labor, laws regulating, 79

Immigration cases, 90-92

Injunction, 1; government by, 265-269

Interstate commerce, 42-55

Interstate Commerce Commission, 43-49

Jefferson, Thomas, on judicial review, 259, 260

Jeopardy, double, under national prohibition, 106-108

Judicial review, 24, 25, 32, 33, 41, 65, 157, 162, 199, 237-264; origin of, 237-240; as applied to acts of Congress, 243-247; as applied to acts of states, 247-254; by state courts, 250, 251; history of attacks upon, 256-258; proposals for curbing, 258-262; courts' attitude toward, 262, 263

Jury trial, 75, 81; in prohibition cases, 100-106

Ju Toy Case, 90, 91, 93

Kent, James, quoted, 163

Labor laws, 78, 79; congressional, declared void, 245, 246

Labor Party, 18

Labor unions, discrimination against, 77, 78

Landis, James, quoted, 267, 270

Laski, Harold, quoted, 234

Lecky, W. E. H., quoted, 163

Lochner v. New York, 258

Lords, House of, powers diminished, 17, 166, 167

Low, Sir Sydney, quoted, 126, 127, 133

Lytton, Lord, quoted, 167

Macaulay, Lord, quoted, 203

[282]

INDEX

McCulloch v. Maryland, 243, 244
McReynolds, J., quoted, 54, 95
Magna Charta, 15, 113
Maine, Sir Henry, quoted, 227
Marbury v. Madison, 240-242, 254
Marshall, John, on judicial review, 240-242; quoted, 259
Merryman Case, 92, 93
Metternich, Prince, quoted, 59
Mill, John Stuart, quoted, 203, 204, 205
Milligan Case, 92
Minimum wage laws, 78, 100
Ministry, see *Cabinet, British*
Moschzisker, J., quoted, 101
Nationalism, and federalism, 58, 59
Ostrogorski, M., quoted, 231, 232
Otis, James, on writs of assistance, 96
Padlock practice, under prohibition, 104-106
Parliamentary government, and presidential distinguished, 114-122; and second chambers, 166, 167; see also *Cabinet*
Paterson, J., quoted, 8
Picketing, 1, 78
Pocket veto, see *President*
Police powers, national, 49-55; of the states, 50
Pollock v. Farmers Loan and Trust Co., 257
President, election of, 26; appointing power of, 26, 151, 156, 157, 174-180; removal power of, 26, 118, 119, 180-194; as chief legislator, 27, 115-118; leadership of, 63, 115-118, 122-124, 130-132; as chief executive, 114, 115, 118-120; responsibility of, to Congress, 134-136; veto power of, 150, 170-174
Presidential government, distinguished from parliamentary, 114-122; assessed, 142-145
Prime Minister, British, choice of, 124-128; see also *Cabinet*

Private rights, see *Bill of rights*
Prohibition, national, 28, 94-108; and states' rights, 66; effect of, on bill of rights, 94-108; convictions under, 102, 103; padlock practice under, 104-106; double jeopardy under, 106-108
Prohibition, state, 53, 54
Proportional representation, 227-232
Proudhon, P. J., quoted, 4
Race segregation, 78
Railroads Shop Crafts Case, 267
Recall of judicial decisions, 258
Removal power, see *President*
Representation, principles of, 163-165; aims of, 202-211; British and American contrasted, 207-209; by geographical districts, 211-227; equality of district populations, 215-227; redistribution of, 217-219; in U. S. Senate, 219-227; proportional, 227-232
Representative government, consent of the governed under, 232-236
Safety appliances laws, 49
Searches and seizures, 75, 82; in prohibition cases, 94-100
Sedition Act of 1798, 82
Senate, power of, over appointing power, 156, 157, 174-180; power of, over treaties, 194-199; representation in, 219-227
Senators, election of, 27
Separation of powers, 120
Spoils system, 208, 209
States, encroachment on powers of, 46-55; not logical units, 59; initiation of measures by, 61, 62
States' rights, doctrine of, 65-71
Story, Joseph, quoted, 8
Supreme Court, five to four decisions by, 1-3, 261-264; an organ of government, 38; see also *Judicial Review*
Sutherland, J., quoted, 263

[283]

INDEX

Taft, William Howard, quoted, 1, 177, 178, 191, 192
Taney, Roger B., quoted, 92, 93
Tenure of Office Act, 182
Toledo Newspaper Company Case, 270
Treason, 74, 84, 85
Treaty making power, 151, 157, 194-199; see also *President*, *Senate*
Unitary government, definition of, 35
United States v. E. C. Knight Company, 256

Versailles, Treaty of, 17, 157, 198
Veto power, see *President, Judicial Review*
Warren, Charles, quoted, 255
Webb, Sidney and Beatrice, quoted, 121, 122
Webster, Daniel, quoted, 255
Wilson, Woodrow, quoted, 227
Woman suffrage, in Great Britain, 17; in the United States, 17
Workmen's compensation laws, 48, 49
Writs of assistance, 96